The Ultimate Amish Guide to Canning and Preserving

Traditional Recipes and Methods for Home Canning and Preservation

Rachel Mast

Table of Contents

Introduction

The Amish people are known for their strong community values and old-fashioned way of living. They believe in hard work and close-knit families. They also believe in establishing a solid connection with the land, and most Amish communities are known for their agricultural practices. They like to cook with what they grow and thus eat hearty old-fashioned meals with their home-grown ingredients. They are some of the best canning and preserving experts worldwide.

Once it is time for harvest, they do their best to preserve whatever they can for the winter and avoid waste. Amish families have passed on their tried and tested recipes through each generation. It's no wonder these recipes have become widely popular amongst other communities worldwide.

Before processed food and modern grocery stores became common, canning was widely practiced in most households. It was a part of life, especially in rural areas. People needed to store food for the winter; the best way to do this was by canning. While this art of food preservation considerably declined in the last few decades, the Amish have continued with the practice.

In recent years, the interest in canning has slowly been growing, and who better to learn from than the Amish? This is why this cookbook was put together with all the best Amish canning recipes for pickles, jams, soups, relishes, and anything you could try home canning with.

Methods of Food Preservation in Amish Homes

Canning

Canning is the primary and preferred method of preserving food in Amish households. They have hundreds of recipes that help them preserve all kinds of food in canning jars. The standard canning method is water bath canning, but many have also started using pressure canning, depending on the food they intend to preserve.

Freezing

The Amish also use freezing as a method of preservation. For most, it is not acceptable to use electricity-powered freezers. This is why blocks of ice play a crucial role in freezing them. They either buy the ice from an ice company or harvest blocks of ice from lakes or ponds nearby if they have access to them. These ice blocks are used in old-fashioned ice boxes or a spring house. These ice boxes work like a freezer usually stored in the basements of Amish homes. They may also transfer their frozen food to a rented commercial locker.

Benefits of Canning and Preserving

Save Money

If one thing can convince anyone to try something new, it's the thought of saving money. Who doesn't like more money in their wallet? With canning, you will save quite a bit on your food bills. Food is more expensive than it has ever been. You can save money by growing your food and canning them. It is especially worth the money when you consider how much better the food quality will be compared to store-bought food.

Eco Friendly

If you want to leave a more positive impact on the environment and reduce your carbon footprint, home canning is one quick step to achieve this. Consuming food you grow or source locally is a great way to reduce your carbon footprint. The other packaged foods you find in stores generally come from miles away, and a lot of fuel and resources are wasted. You will also not be adding to the enormous piles of packaging waste.

Better Health

Processed or store-bought canned food contains a lot of harmful preservatives and additives. You know exactly how you will preserve the food with home canning. You can avoid using harmful ingredients and all the excess sugar in commercial canning. Home canning is the healthier choice.

Avoid Waste

One of the main reasons why canning was started in the first place was to preserve food. What will you do with the produce if you live alone or grow more than your family needs? You can only eat so much in a day or even a week. The next best thing is to preserve the food by home canning. This way, you don't have to waste any food and will also have delicious food to enjoy throughout the year.

Better Flavors

Everyone knows that homemade food tastes better. This applies to home-canned food as well. When you make canned goods using home-grown or locally bought produce, they will be of higher quality. You also have the chance to tweak recipes and get the exact taste that you or your family prefers. This makes canning worth the effort. You get healthier and tastier products when you practice home canning.

Source of Income

You can always sell your canned products to make a little extra money. When you have too much produce and more cans of food than you need, the best thing to do is sell them. You can talk to your local grocery store or sell them at the farmers market. People are always looking for better-tasting and healthy homemade goods.

Gifting

Canned goods are great for gifting. In a time when people barely put effort and time into their relationships, you can give them a symbol of this. Use some decorative jars and labels for your gifting cans. It could be anything from jams to pickles that the receiving person enjoys. It will save you money and will be a more appreciated gift.

Stay Prepared

Canning is also a great way to prepare for hard times. It could be a financial crisis when you struggle to buy groceries. It could also be an emergency where all the grocery stores are closed, or you can't leave the house because of a crisis. In such times, your pantry full of canned goods will help you and the family survive. This is why a lot of survivalists spend time learning home canning. You never know when such situations may occur, and the best thing to do is be prepared.

If nothing else, canning is fun! It's a great hobby to take up and also an enjoyable way to spend time with others. Try getting everyone involved and make it a family activity. You can also do it with your friends on the weekend! Now you have enough reasons to begin home canning like the Amish!

Canning can be carried out at home using water bath and pressure canning. Traditionally, the Amish people only used water bath canning to preserve their food. However, many also use pressure canning since it allows them to preserve low-acid foods. Since food safety is very important, it is best to use the best method for safe food preservation. A pressure canner is considered a modern convenience, but it is one of the few for which they have started making allowances. Water bath and pressure canning should be learned since they have unique uses.

Methods of Canning

Water Bath Canning

Water bath canning is a very old method of preserving food. While many people previously used this method to preserve every food, it is appropriate only for high-acid foods. The acidity of the food plays a critical role in water bath canning. The acidity will kill harmful bacteria that usually spoil the food or cause botulism.

Foods that can be preserved safely by water bath canning include fresh tomatoes, fruits, fruit juices, salsas, pickles, relishes, vinegar, condiments, jams, and jellies.

Pressure Canning

Pressure canning is the best method for preserving any low-acid foods you want to store in cans. The canning jars are heated to 240 ° F. This high temperature kills harmful bacteria that would cause spoilage in the canned food.

Foods that can be preserved safely by pressure canning include potatoes, corn, carrots, sweet peppers, meats, beets, pumpkins, green beans, and other greens.

The process of canning may vary depending on the food product. For instance, some fruits must be pitted or peeled before they may be canned. Some veggies need to be treated with heat before they can be used for canning. Meats or fish must be cooked first, and the bones removed before canning. Some types of fish also have to be shelled.

Similarly, the exact canning process will vary depending on the foods you plan to prepare. Generally, dairy products such as eggs, milk, and cheese should not be preserved by canning. It is also recommended that you don't try canning any thick purees since they may not get heated evenly to the right temperature. Heating is important in killing bacteria, which is not always possible with thick purees. Such foods can be preserved by freezing instead. Avoid canning flour, cornstarch, and arrowroot powder as well. These ingredients should only be used in canning recipes if they are specifically mentioned and are from a trusted recipe source.

Tips for Home Canning

Always Follow the Proper Recipe

Until you become a canning expert and have invented your recipes, follow the tried and tested recipes passed down. Follow all the steps mentioned in the recipe, from the processing time to the amount of space you should leave at the top of the jar. This headspace is important in canning since it expands the food and allows bubbling during the canning process. Keeping this head space in mind is important to ensure proper sealing of the canning jars.

Always Wash and Clean Your Canning Equipment

Keep everything from your knife and cutting board to the canner clean. Wash and store them after every use. Sterilize the canning equipment before you start canning anything. This will help avoid any spoilage from germs or dirt on the equipment. 'To sterilize your canning jars and lids, place them in boiling water for 10 minutes. You can then drain and use them for canning.

Try to Use Produce That Is Ripe and Not Damaged for Canning

The purpose of canning is to preserve the food for safe consumption later. If you use to produce that is already spoiling, the bacteria in that little damaged part can spoil the entire can of food.

So, if you want an excellent finished product, start with the best produce in the beginning.

All Your Produce Should be Washed and Cleaned

Depending on where you get your produce, there could be any number of bacteria or parasites on them. It is best to wash the produce in warm water with a little food-safe detergent. Wash this off with clean water again. This will help eliminate many food contaminants before you begin canning.

Equipment Required for Canning

Canning Jars

Canning jars come in different shapes and sizes. The ones used in home canning are made from glass and are built explicitly for this purpose. Buy these in bulk to get them at the best rates. You can also choose between the wide-mouth and narrow-mouth jars. Choose the sizes according to what or how much food you want to store in the jars. Quart jars are usually best for storing any canned fruits, meat, or vegetables. You can use pint jars for storing your jellies, jams, and pickles. Half-pint jars are good for storing food like relishes you use a little at once.

Canning Lids and Rings

When you buy canning jars, they come with their lids. However, you cannot reuse these lids, and the jars must be sealed with new lids whenever you can get food again. So, buy extra lids and make sure they fit your jars. You will also need rings, which usually come with canning jars. You don't need to buy extra rings since these are unscrewed after sealing the jars and rarely go bad. Just keep a few extra rings in store.

Tongs

Tongs are a great tool to add ingredients to your cans. Keep a clean pair of kitchen tongs made of stainless steel for your canning activities.

Water Bath Canner

A water bath canner is a necessity for canning any high-acid foods. You can also use a stockpot as an alternative but getting a proper water bath canner is more appropriate.

Pressure Canner

A good pressure canner will last you a long time. You will need this for canning and low-acid foods. Unless you belong to a very strict Amish household, you can generally get a pressure canner for your kitchen and a water bath canner.

Measuring Tools

One of the most critical parts about canning is that you will usually have to follow all the recipes as accurately as possible. This is why you need a few different measuring cups and spoons. You can use them to measure all the ingredients out and add them while preparing your food. This leaves no room for error and will help you avoid wastage from an improper recipe.

Weighing Scale

A weighing scale will help you measure your ingredients and follow any canning recipes as accurately as possible.

Funnel

Buy a narrow-mouth and wide-mouth funnel for canning. This is one of those tools that you will constantly be using. It will help you get every bit of food into the cans and avoid any spillage or wastage.

Ladle

A ladle, like tongs, will be handy in adding ingredients to your cans. A sterilized steel ladle will allow you to scoop any soups, jams, and relishes cleanly into your canning jars. You don't want to struggle with small spoons or ladles that you usually use for cooking since they will only make a mess.

Labels

Canning helps increase your food's shelf life, but nothing can last forever. Labeling your cans and storing them in the pantry will help you avoid spoilage. Always label your canning jars with the exact date of canning and estimated expiry date. This way, you can use up the older jars before opening the jars that will keep well. You can also get decorative labels for canned goods you want to give or sell.

Jar Lifter

A jar lifter is a convenient tool. It will allow you to safely lift your canning jars from the hot water bath once they have been sealed. This is much more convenient than struggling with oven mitts or kitchen towels to pick up the jars without burning yourself.

Safety Tips

- Don't eat canned food if you notice any of the following:
- Discoloration, mold growth, or a foul smell from the food.
- If the container or lid looks like it is bulging or swollen.
- If there is foam or liquid spurting once the can is opened.
- Cracks or damage on the canning jars.

Botulism

This is one of the most significant risks to consider regarding canned food. It is caused by clostridium botulinum, a bacteria that is found everywhere. Food-borne botulism can be deadly or cause food poisoning, paralysis, etc. It is tough to detect the spores since they are not visible to the naked eye. However, these bacteria are killed if you follow the proper canning process. The bacteria thrive in a damp environment with no oxygen, so canning jars are perfect for them. To prevent botulism, following the canning process accurately is essential while keeping all safety measures in mind.

Learn about Acidity

The acidic levels of food play an essential role in canning. Learn about the different pH levels of different foods. This will help you determine whether you should use water bath canning or pressure canning for safe food preservation. You will also know whether you need to use any other ingredients in your recipes to best preserve the food.

All Canning Equipment Is Different

You can't follow the same instructions for every canner. They are all made differently, and you should pay attention to the instructions for your canner. Take time to get familiar with your equipment so you can use it properly and ensure food safety during canning. The manufacturer may also recommend specific types of jars or lids that work best with your canner.

Don't Improvise

Trying new recipes can be extremely fun, but this is not always a good idea with canning. You should follow the recipes as thoroughly as possible. You can try your improvisations over time when you learn more about canning.

Always Check the Seals

Once you finish scanning your jars, always check the seals. If the jars are not sealed properly, repeat the canning process and seal them again. Improperly sealed jars will always cause spoilage.

With all this information in mind, you are ready to start trying all the fantastic Amish canning recipes in this book!

Water Bath Canning Procedure

ollow the manufacturer's instructions on operating the water bath canner. You must prepare the canner, jars, lids, and bands for canning the jars. The jars, lids, and bands need to be sterilized.

1. First, clean the jars and 2-part lids (lids and bands) with a soap solution. Rinse them in hot water.
2. Fill up the water bath canner or a deep pot with water. Place the jars in, ensuring the water is at least an inch over the top of the jar lids.
3. If you have a jar rack, place it in the canner. If not, place any rack in there, ensuring the jars do not touch the bottom of the canner directly.
4. Place the jars on the rack and submerge them in the water. Place the pot over high heat, and when it starts boiling, let it boil for about 8 – 10 minutes.
5. Turn the heat to low. Let the water simmer until you need the jars.
6. If the lids and rings are of the new type that is currently available, you need not simmer them. If the lids and rings are of the old type, put them in a saucepan of water and let it simmer on low heat on another burner.
7. When the food to be canned is ready, spread a clean kitchen towel on your countertop.
8. Use a jar lifter to remove the jars from the pot w and place them on the towel.
9. Wipe the rims and jars with a clean cloth. Fill the jars with the food that is to be canned. Use the help of a wide-mouth funnel while adding food or liquid into the jars.
10. When you fill the jars, make sure to leave some space on top of the jars over the filling. This space is called headspace.

Generally, about ¼ to ½ inch of headspace is required in the jars.

11. Remove the air bubbles from the filled jars. Take a blunt knife, a bubbleremoving tool, or a plastic spatula to remove the air bubbles. Simply put the knife into the jars and move it around for a few seconds so that any bubbles are removed. By doing this, the headspace may reduce. You have to reassess the headspace. If the headspace has reduced, add more food or liquid (according to the recipe) into the jars to get the required headspace.

12. Take a clean damp cloth and wipe the rim of the jars. Lift the canning lids, one at a time, using a lid lifter, and place the canning lid on each jar. Place the canning ring on each jar and tighten it- finger tight but not very tight.

13. Pick the jars with the jar lifter and place the jars in the canner on the rack.

14. Make sure the jars do not touch each other. They will not touch each other if you are using a jar rack. It can happen on a regular rack.

15. Next, check if the jars are completely submerged in the water and there is at least an inch of water above the top of the jars.

16. If the water is not at least 1 inch on top of the jars, boil some water and pour it into the canner.

17. Close the lid of the water bath canner. Turn up the heat to high heat once again.

18. When the water starts boiling, start the timer and let it boil for the required time mentioned in the recipe. For example, if it is mentioned in the recipe "Process for 10 minutes," - it means when the water starts boiling, start the timer for 10 minutes.

19. The processing time is different for different foods.

20. The timing given in each recipe is for canning at sea level and up to 1000 feet.

21. If you live at higher altitudes beyond 1000 feet, you must add extra time to the time mentioned in the recipes.

22. Add 1-minute extra time for every 1000 feet beyond the first 1000 feet.
23. When the timer goes off, let the jars remain in the canner for 8 – 10 minutes. Do not open the lid of the canner.
24. Now remove the lid and lift the jars out with the help of the jar lifter. Lift them straight without tilting.
25. Place the jars on the towel. Do not check for the seals now. Let them rest for 12 to 24 hours, as mentioned in the recipe. After about an hour of resting, you may hear a "pop" or a" ping" sound. That is perfectly ok. The jars are getting appropriately sealed, and the lids may be slightly concave as they get sucked into the jars.
26. While the jars are resting, ensure you do not disturb their jars.
27. Once the resting time is over, you can check for the seals. The lid should not move if you press it. If some jar is not sealed correctly, place them in the refrigerator and use them within 2 – 3 weeks.
28. Stick a label on the jars with the name and date of making. Store the jars in a cool and dark place. Most recipes last for at least a year unless specified in the recipe.
29. Whenever you open a jar, make sure to keep the jar in the refrigerator if there are leftovers.
30. So, this procedure will not be mentioned in every recipe.

Water Bath Canning Recipes

Chokecherry Jelly

Yields: 4 – 5 half-pint jars

Ingredients:

- 1 1/2 pounds of chokecherries
- 3 tablespoons liquid pectin
- 3 1/4 cups sugar
- 1/8 teaspoon almond extract

Directions:

1. Place chokecherries into a pot and crush them with a potato masher. Pour enough water to cover the chokecherries.
2. Place the pot over medium-high heat. When the mixture starts boiling, turn the heat to low heat and cook until the berries are soft.
3. Place 4 layers of cheesecloth over a strainer and place it over a bowl. Pour the berries into the strainer.
4. Let the juice strain for about 30 minutes. The berries are no longer needed in this recipe. Measure the strained juice; it should be about 1 1/2 cups. If the juice doesn't measure up to 1 1/2 cups, add water to get 1 1/2 cups.
5. Add strained juice and sugar into a pot and cook over high heat. Stir constantly until the sugar melts.
6. When the mixture starts boiling, stir in the pectin. Let the mixture start boiling once again. Let it boil rapidly for precisely 1 minute, and then turn off the heat. Remove any scum that may be on the surface. Stir for a couple of minutes.
7. Stir in the almond extract.
8. Pour the jelly into the prepared jars, leaving a 1/4 inch of headspace from the rim of the jars. Seal the jars after debubbling.
9. Process the jars in the prepared canner for 5 minutes, adjusting for altitude if required.

☆ ☆ ☆ ☆ ☆

Violet Jelly

Yields: 3 half-pint jars

Ingredients:

- 2 – 2 1/4 cups water
- 1 tablespoon lemon juice
- 1 1/2 cups lightly packed wild violet flowers
- 1 box (2 ounces) of pectin powder
- 1 1/2 cups granulated sugar

Directions:

1. Start by placing the violet flowers in a saucepan.
2. Boil some water, pour it over the flowers, and ensure that they are covered with water. Cover the saucepan and set aside for 24 hours in a cool area.
3. Strain the mixture into a bowl and discard the flowers.
4. Measure the tea; you need 1 3/4 cup of violet tea. If it does not measure 1 3/4 cups, add more water.
5. Add violet tea and lemon juice into the saucepan and stir.
6. Place the pot over high heat and bring it to a boil.
7. Add sugar and pectin, and using a wooden spoon, stir the mixture. Once the sugar dissolves completely, allow the mixture to come to a boil. Let it boil for precisely 1 minute, then turn off the heat. Discard any scum that rises on top.
8. Pour the jelly into the prepared jars, leaving a headspace of 1/4 inch. Remove the bubbles. Seal the jars.
9. Put the jars in the prepared canner and process for 5 minutes, adjusting for altitude if required.

☆ ☆ ☆ ☆ ☆

Rosehip and Apple Jelly

Yields: 2 – 3 half-pint jars

Ingredients:

- 1/2 quart rose hips
- 1 1/2 cups sugar
- 2 medium tart apples, cored, peeled, chopped
- 0.45 ounce powdered pectin
- 2 – 3 drops of red food coloring (optional)
- A pinch ground mace (optional)

Directions:

1. Place the rose hips in a Dutch oven or pot, and mash them lightly with a potato masher. Pour enough water to just cover, and place the pot over high heat.
2. When the mixture starts boiling, turn the heat to low heat and cook for about 5 minutes.
3. Place 4 layers of cheesecloth over a strainer and place it over a bowl. Pour the mixture into the strainer.
4. Let the juice strain for about 30 minutes. The rose hips are no longer needed. Set aside the juice.
5. Now, add apples to the Dutch oven. Pour enough water to cover the apples and place them over medium heat.
6. When the mixture starts boiling, bring down the heat to low and cook for about 5 minutes.
7. Pour the mixture into the strainer and strain the juice. Discard the apples.
8. Measure the strained juices (both rosehip juice and apple juice). You need 1/2 cup of rose hip juice and 3/4 cup of apple juice. If it does not measure this much, pour enough water to get the required quantity.
9. Pour the juice into the pot. Place the pot over high heat and bring it to a boil. Add the food coloring if using.
10. Stir in sugar and pectin. with a wooden spoon. Keep on

stirring until the sugar dissolves completely, and allow the mixture to come to a boil. Let it rapidly boil for precisely 1 minute., then turn the heat off and discard any scum that appears on top. Add mace and stir.

11. Pour the jelly into the prepared jars, leaving 1/4 inch of empty space on top. Seal the jars after debubbling.

12. The jars are to be processed in the prepared canner for 5 minutes. Adjust the timing for altitude if necessary.

Dandelion Jelly

Yields: 4 half-pints or 2-pint jars

Ingredients:

- 1 2/3 cups water
- 1 tablespoon lemon juice
- 2 cups lightly packed dandelion petals (use large, dry, and bright yellow petals)
- 1/2 package (from a 1.75-ounce package) of pectin powder
- 2 1/4 cups granulated sugar
- A drop of yellow food coloring

Directions:

1. Combine water and dandelion petals in a saucepan and place it over medium heat.

2. When it begins to boil, turn the heat to low heat and cook for 9 – 10 minutes.

3. Place a strainer over a bowl and pour the mixture into the strainer. Strain the mixture and press the petals with the back of a spoon to get maximum liquid.

4. You need 1 1/2 cups of dandelion tea. If it does not measure 1 1/2 cups, add some water to make it 1 1/2 cups. If there is extra, you can enjoy the dandelion tea by adding some honey

to it.

5. Add the measured dandelion tea, lemon juice, food coloring, and pectin into a pot and stir.

6. Place the pot over high heat and bring it to a boil. Add in the sugar and stir the mixture using a wooden spoon. Once the sugar dissolves completely, allow the mixture to come to a boil once again. Let it boil for exactly a minute. Turn off the heat. Remove any foam that floats on the surface.

7. Pour the jelly into the prepared jars, leaving a headspace of 1/4 inch. Remove the bubbles before sealing the jars.

8. Process the jars in the prepared canner for 5 minutes, adjusting for altitude if required.

Pomegranate Jelly

Yields: 5 – 6 half-pint size jars

Ingredients:

- 3 3/4 cups white sugar
- Juice of a lemon
- 2 cups pomegranate juice
- 3 ounces liquid pectin

Directions:

1. To make pomegranate juice. Take about 3 – 4 cups of fresh pomegranate arils and put them into a juicer. Extract the juice and measure out 2 cups of the juice. If it doesn't measure 2 cups, add enough water to make it 2 cups.

2. Add sugar, lemon juice, and pomegranate juice into a stainless steel saucepan and place the saucepan over high heat. Stir often until the sugar dissolves completely.

3. When it starts boiling, add pectin and stir until well combined. When it comes to a boil once again, allow it to boil rapidly for

precisely 30 seconds and no longer. Turn off the heat.

4. Remove any scum that has risen to the surface of the liquid. Turn off the heat.

5. Pour the jelly into the prepared jars, leaving an empty space of 1/4 inch on top of the jars. Seal the jars after removing the bubbles.

6. Process the jars in the prepared canner for 5 minutes, adjusting for altitude if required.

Clover Blossom Jelly

Yields: 3 half-pint jars

Ingredients:

- 2 cups clover blossoms, rinsed
- 2 cups sugar
- 1/2 package of liquid pectin
- 2 cups boiling water
- 2 tablespoons lemon juice

Directions:

1. To make clover blossom tea: Place clover blossoms in a bowl. Pour 2 cups boiling water over the flowers. Cover the bowl and set aside for 45 minutes to steep. Stir every 15 minutes.

2. Place a strainer over a bowl and strain the mixture. Now measure the tea. You should get a cup of tea. If it doesn't measure 1 cup, pour enough water to make it 1 cup. Pour the tea into a saucepan over medium heat and add the lemon juice and sugar.

3. Raise heat to medium-high heat. Keep stirring and bring to a boil.

4. Stir in pectin and continue boiling for a couple of minutes. Turn off the heat.

5. Meanwhile, place a saucer in the freezer for 8 – 10 minutes to test if the jelly is ready.

6. Take out the saucer from the freezer and drop a teaspoon of the jelly mixture over it.

7. In a couple of minutes, touch the jelly and see if it is your desired consistency. Make sure you do not cook it too much, as it will also set in the jars.

8. If you want it thicker, continue simmering for a minute or two and not longer.

9. Remove any scum that is floating on top of the liquid. Turn off the heat.

10. Transfer the jelly to the prepared jars. Leave 1/4 inch of empty space on top of the jars. Debubble and seal the jars.

11. Place the jars in the prepared canner and process for 10 minutes. Adjust for altitude if required.

Water Bath Canning Syrup Recipes

Elderflower Syrup

Yields: 1 quart or 2-pint jars

Ingredients:

- 10 – 15 elderflower umbels, rinsed, cut into small florets, discard stems (try to use the cream-colored umbels)
- 1/2 quart water
- Juice of 2 lemons
- Zest of 2 lemons, grated
- 2 1/4 cups sugar

Directions:

1. Combine elderflowers, lemon juice, and lemon zest in a glass bowl.
2. Add water and sugar into a pot and place the pot over medium heat. Stir frequently until the sugar dissolves completely.
3. When it starts boiling, turn off the heat.
4. Pour the sugar syrup over the elderflowers. Mix well and cover the bowl with a lid. Set aside on your countertop for 3 – 5 days.
5. Line a strainer with cheesecloth. Place the strainer over a bowl. Pour the syrup into the strainer and strain the syrup.
6. Pour the strained syrup into a saucepan. Place the saucepan over medium heat and bring to a boil. Turn off the heat.
7. Pour the syrup into the prepared jars. 1 There should be a headspace of 1/4 inch. After removing the bubbles, seal the jars.
8. The jars are to be processed in the prepared canner for 10 minutes, adjusting for altitude if required.
9. To serve: Serve with seltzer, club soda, white wine, or vodka. You can also serve it with ice cream, frozen yogurt, or yogurt.

Blueberry Syrup

Yields: 1 quart or 4-pint jars

Ingredients:

- 8 cups ripe, rinsed fresh blueberries (measure after discarding the stems)
- 1 cup corn syrup
- 6 cups sugar
- 4 tablespoons lemon juice
- 2 teaspoons vanilla extract (optional)

Directions:

1. Place the berries in a saucepan, and crush them lightly with a potato masher. Place the saucepan over medium-high heat and bring to a boil. Turn the heat to medium-low heat and cook for about 2 minutes. Stir often.
2. Turn off the heat. Place a colander over a bowl, pour the berries into the colander and strain the juice.
3. Place 2 layers of cheesecloth over a strainer and place it over a bowl. Pour the strained juice into the strainer.
4. Let the juice strain for about 30 minutes. The berries are no longer needed. You should get around 5 cups of juice.
5. Combine corn syrup, sugar, lemon juice, and blueberry juice in a saucepan.
6. Add blueberries. Let it boil rapidly for precisely 1 minute. Stir continuously. Scrape the bottom of the saucepan while stirring.
7. Turn off the heat. Add vanilla and stir.
8. Pour the syrup into the jars, leaving a headspace of 1/4 inch. Remove the bubbles. Seal the jars.
9. Process the jars in the prepared canner for 10 minutes, adjusting for altitude if required.
10. To serve: Seltzer, club soda, white wine, or vodka is a great choice to serve the syrup. You can also serve it with ice cream,

frozen yogurt, or yogurt.

Peach Syrup

Yields: 3-pint jars

Ingredients:

- 3 1/2 cups prepared fresh or frozen peaches or nectarines (measure after pitting and peeling, and chopping- the procedure is given below)
- 2 cups sugar
- 2 tablespoons lemon juice

Directions:

1. If you have a juicer, juice the peaches in the juicer. Continue from step 9.
2. If you do not have a juicer, boil a pot over high heat. When water starts boiling, drop peaches in the boiling water. Drain off after 30 – 60 seconds and not longer. Blanching makes peeling easier.
3. Drain in a colander and immediately put the peaches in a bowl of cold water. This stops further cooking.
4. Peel the skin off the peaches.
5. Cut the peaches into small pieces. Measure 3 1/2 cups of peaches and put them into a heavy pot.
6. Pour about 2 inches of water over the peaches. Cover the pot and place it over medium high heat. Cook until soft.
7. Place a strainer over a bowl and line it with 2 layers of cheesecloth. Pour the peaches into the strainer and strain the juice. Do not press the peaches; you can stir them gently a couple of times. Let it strain for about 30 minutes. You need about 2 – 2 1/2 cups of juice.
8. If you want to make low-sugar syrup, reduce some of the sugar

and add some Splenda or stevia, or Truvia.

9. Add peach juice, sugar, and lemon juice into a pot and place the pot over high heat.

10. Cook until the syrup is thickened, as per your preference. Remove any foam that rises to the surface. Turn off the heat.

11. Transfer the syrup into the prepared jars, leaving a headspace of 1/2 inch. Remove the bubbles. Seal the jars.

12. Place the jars in the canner and process for 10 minutes, adjusting for altitude if required.

Plum Syrup

Yields: 3-pint jars

Ingredients:

- 2 1/2 cups fresh plum juice
- 2 1/2 cups sugar
- 2 tablespoons lemon juice

Directions:

1. Add plum juice, sugar, and lemon juice into a pot and place the pot over high heat.

2. Cook until the syrup is thickened, as per your preference. Remove any foam that floats on top. Turn off the heat.

3. Pour the syrup into the prepared jars, leaving an empty space of 1/2 inch on top of the jars. Remove the bubbles before sealing the jars.

4. Process the jars in the prepared canner for 10 minutes, adjusting for altitude if required.

Prickly Pear Syrup

Yields: 2 pints

Ingredients:

- 2 pounds prickly pears
- 2 cups sugar or as required
- Water as required
- 2 teaspoons citric acid

Directions:

1. Place the prickly pears in a pot, and pour just enough water to cover them. Cover the pot over high heat, and allow it to boil; remove from heat.
2. Let it sit covered for 30 minutes.
3. Mash the prickly pears using a potato masher. Transfer the mixture to a food mill to strain the seeds. Discard the seeds.
4. Place a fine wire mesh strainer over a bowl. Pour the strained prickly pears into the strainer and strain the juice. Discard the solids.
5. Line the strainer with cheesecloth and strain the mixture once again.
6. Pour the strained juice into a measuring cup and measure the juice. You should be having around 2 cups of strained juice.
7. Add the same quantity of sugar, i.e., 2 cups. If the juice is less or more, add sugar accordingly.
8. Combine prickly pear juice and sugar in a pot. Place the pot over medium heat. Stir often until the sugar dissolves completely.
9. When the mixture starts boiling, turn the heat to low heat and let it gently boil for about 3 – 4 minutes. Remove from heat and let the syrup sit for 15 minutes. Add half the citric acid and stir until well combined. Taste a bit of it. If you like the taste, do not add the remaining citric acid, or else add the remaining citric acid and mix well.

10. The syrup is to be poured into the jars. Leave a headspace of 1/2 inch. Debubble before sealing the jars.

11. Place the jars for processing in the prepared canner for 10 minutes., Adjust for altitude if required.

12. To serve: Mix 1 to 2 tablespoons of the syrup in a glass of chilled water. Add some crushed ice and serve. You can also use it as a topping for fruit salad or desserts or make cocktails and mocktails.

Water Bath Canning Jam

Apricot Pineapple Jam

Yields: 2 – 3 half-pint jars

Ingredients:

- 1 1/2 cups mashed apricots
- 2 tablespoons bottled lemon juice
- 1/4 to 1/2 cup honey or 1/2 - 1 cup sugar
- 1/2 cup crushed, canned pineapple, drained
- 2 teaspoons calcium water (that comes with Pomona pectin powder)
- 1 1/2 teaspoons Pomona's pectin powder

Directions:

1. To make calcium water: Measure 1/4 teaspoon of calcium powder that comes in the box of Pomona's pectin and put it into a small jar. Mix it up with 1/4 cup of water, fasten the lid on, and shake the jar constantly until well incorporated. You will only need 2 teaspoons of calcium water for this recipe so store the rest in the refrigerator. It can be used later to make another batch of jelly or jam.
2. Add apricots, pineapple, lemon juice, and calcium water into a saucepan and mix well. Place the saucepan over high heat. Stir often until the sugar dissolves completely.
3. Meanwhile, mix pectin powder and sugar or honey in a bowl.
4. When the apricot mixture starts boiling, stir in the pectin mixture. Stir constantly for a couple of minutes.
5. When the mixture comes to a rapid boil, turn off the heat.
6. Pour the jam into the jars. Make sure to leave 1/4 inch of empty space at the rim of the jar. Remove the bubbles. Seal the jars.
7. Place the jars in the prepared canner and process for 10 minutes., Adjust for altitude if necessary.

Berry Jam

Yields: 3 – 4 half-pint jars

Ingredients:

- 3 cups granulated sugar
- 4 1/2 cups crushed berries
- 1/4 teaspoon butter (optional but recommended to reduce foaming)

Directions:

1. Place berries in a bowl. Mash them with a potato masher. If you want to remove all the seeds or remove the seeds partially, add the berries (all berries or some berries) into a food mill and strain the berries. Discard the solids.
2. Now measure 4 1/2 cups of berries and add them to a pot.
3. Stir in the remaining berries (if removing the seeds partially) and sugar, and cook the mixture over high heat.
4. When the berries start boiling, add butter and stir.
5. Turn the heat to medium and cook for about 15 minutes. Stir the berries often.
6. Cook until the mixture's temperature is about 220 degrees F at sea level or slightly lower than at higher altitudes. Minus 1 degree F for every 500 feet height above sea level. Suppose you are a height of 2000 feet; the mixture's temperature should be 216 degrees F when the jam is ready. Stir often and then turn off the heat. Discard any scum that may be on the surface of the mixture every few minutes.
7. Ladle the jam into jars. Headspace of 1/4 inch is to be left from the rim. Remove bubbles before sealing the jars.
8. Put the jars in the water bath canner for 10 minutes, adjusting for altitude if required.

Damson Plum Jam

Yields: 8 half-pint jars

Ingredients:

- 9 cups damson plum pulp
- 5 cups sugar, granulated
- Juice of a lemon
- Zest of a lemon, grated
- 2 pouches of liquid pectin

Directions:

1. In a large, non-reactive pot, add the sugar and the fruit pulp. Mix well.
2. Let this mixture cook over high heat until it starts bubbling.
3. Once the mixture starts bubbling, add lemon juice and lemon zest and mix well.
4. Let the mixture cook for around 20 minutes until the jam looks thick, shiny, and glossy.
5. Add pectin to the mixture and stir well. Let it boil for five more minutes.
6. Remove the pot from heat.
7. Put dollops of jam into the jars. Leave 1/2 inch of space at the top of the jars. Make sure to remove the bubbles before sealing the jars.
8. Place the jars in a water bath canner and process for 10 minutes. Adjust the time for higher altitudes if required.

Blueberry Jam

Yields: 6 half-pint jars

Ingredients:

- 6 cups blueberries, crushed and mashed

- 3 1/2 cups sugar, granulated
- Juice and zest of 1 lemon
- 1/2 teaspoons nutmeg, freshly ground
- 2 teaspoons cinnamon, ground
- 2 packs of liquid pectin

Directions:

1. Add sugar and mashed blueberries to a large, non-reactive pot. Mix well.
2. Let this mixture boil over high heat until it starts bubbling.
3. When the mixture starts bubbling, add cinnamon, lemon juice, lemon zest, and nutmeg and mix well.
4. Let the mixture cook for around 20 minutes or until the jam looks thick, shiny, and glossy.
5. Add pectin to the mixture. Give it a good stir and let it boil for five more minutes.
6. Remove the pot from the heat.
7. Fill the jam into the jars. Leave 1/2 inch of space at the top of the jars. Make sure to debubble before sealing the jars.
8. Put the jars in a water bath canner and process for 10 minutes. Adjust for altitude if required.

Lime and Nectarine Jam

Yields: 4-pint jars

Ingredients:

- 3 cups sugar, granulated
- 6 cups chopped and pitted nectarines
- Juice and zest from 3 medium-sized lemons
- 1 packet of liquid pectin

Directions:

1. Add sugar and nectarine into a non-reactive pot and mix well.

Set it aside for about 20 minutes. Allow the nectarine to release its juices to combine with sugar well. The mixture should be soft enough to be mashed with a wooden spoon. Now mash the mixture.

2. Place this pot on high heat and let it boil for a few minutes. Stir often. Remove the foam on the surface from time to time.

3. After about 20 minutes, add pectin, lemon juice, and zest to the pot and mix well. Let the mixture boil for another five minutes. The mixture should ideally look like molten lava.

4. For chunky jam, leave the mixture as it is. You may blend the mixture with an immersion or a regular blender for smoother jams.

5. Take the pot off the heat and spoon the jam into the jars. Make sure to leave 1/2 inch of empty space on top of the jars. Also, remove the air bubbles.

6. Let the jars boil in a water bath for 10 minutes. Make sure to adjust the timing for higher altitudes.

7. Store in a cool and dark place. It should look thick and spreadable.

Easy-Peasy Raspberry Jam

Yields: 4-pint jars

Ingredients:

- 4 cups sugar, granulated
- 7 cups raspberries, crushed
- Juice and zest of 1 lemon
- 1 pouch of liquid pectin

Directions:

1. In a different saucepan, add all the lids and let them simmer in water on low heat. The heat should be as low as possible.

2. In another non-reactive pot, combine sugar and raspberries. Let the mixture cook for around 20 minutes until the mixture can be mashed with the back of a wooden spoon.

3. Mash the mixture. Add lemon zest, juice, and pectin to the mixture and mix well. Allow the mixture to cook for at least 5 minutes. Turn off the heat.

4. For smoother jams, blend the mixture using an immersion blender. For chunky jam, use it as it is.

5. Take the pot off the heat and put dollops of jam in the jars. Leave headspace of 1/2 inch.

6. Place the jars in the water bath canner and process for 10 minutes. Adjust for altitude if necessary.

Peach, Plum, and Ginger Jam

Yields: 4-pint jars

Ingredients:

- 5 cups pitted, peeled, crushed peaches
- 3 cups pitted, mashed plums
- 4 cups sugar, granulated
- 3/4 cup ginger juice

Directions:

1. Add peaches, plums, sugar, and ginger juice into a pot. Place the pot over high heat.

2. Let it cook for about 20 minutes. Remove scum from the top of the mixture.

3. Turn off the heat. Spoon the jam into the jars, leaving 1/2 inch of space on top of the jars.

4. After removing the bubbles, seal the jars.

5. Put the jars in the boiling water bath and process for 10 minutes. The timing is to be changed for higher altitudes.

Cantaloupe and Vanilla Jam

Yields: 3-pint jars

Ingredients:

- 5 cups cantaloupe, peeled, deseeded, chopped
- 2 vanilla beans, split, scraped
- 2 tablespoons lemon juice, freshly squeezed
- 3 cups sugar, granulated
- Zest of 2 lemons, grated
- 2 pouches (3 ounces each) of liquid pectin

Directions:

1. Add sugar, cantaloupe, and vanilla bean seeds and pods into a stainless steel pot or saucepan.
2. Place the pot over high heat. Mix well. Let this mixture boil for around 8-10 minutes.
3. Stir in liquid pectin, lemon zest, and lemon juice. Let the mixture come to a boil. Let the mixture boil rapidly for another 3-4 minutes. The mixture should look thick and bubbly. Stir often.
4. Once the mixture has thickened, remove the vanilla pod and discard it. Turn off the heat.
5. Fill the jam into the jars. Make sure to leave a space of 1/4 inch on top of the jars, removing bubbles.
6. Process the jars in the prepared canner for 10 minutes. Adjust for altitude if required.

Fig Jam

Yields: 6 half-pint jars

Ingredients:

- 7 cups fresh figs, coarsely chopped
- Juice of 2 lemons
- 4 cups sugar, granulated
- 1 pack of liquid pectin

Directions:

1. Add sugar and the chopped figs into a stainless steel saucepan. Mix well.
2. Place the mixture over high heat. Stir on and off until the mixture comes to a boil.
3. Once the mixture starts boiling, add lemon juice and mix well.
4. Let the mixture cook for around 20 minutes or until the jam is thick. Stir on and off.
5. Add pectin to the mixture and give it a good stir.
6. Let it cook for another 5 minutes.
7. Ladle the jam into the jars, leaving a space of 1/4 inch on the top of the jar. After removing the bubbles, seal the jars.
8. Place the jars in the boiling water bath and boil for 10 minutes, adjusting the time for altitude if required.

Rhubarb, Orange, and Strawberry Jam

Yields: 6-pint jars

Ingredients:

- 8 cups rhubarb chopped (around 3 pounds)
- 6 cups strawberries, chopped (around 3 dry pints)
- Juice of 3 oranges

- Zest of 3 oranges, grated
- 6 cups granulated sugar
- 1 teaspoon ground cinnamon
- 2 1/2 packets of liquid pectin

Directions:

1. Combine the rhubarb, strawberries, orange juice, orange zest, sugar, and cinnamon, and mix well. Put this pot on low heat and let it simmer after it comes to a boil.
2. The mixture should cook at medium heat for 20 minutes. The rhubarb should break down.
3. Once the rhubarb has broken down, add pectin to the mixture and stir well.
4. Turn up the heat to high heat. Let the mixture boil for 5 minutes.
5. Remove the pot from heat and fill the jars with the prepared jam.
6. Fill the jars with jam. Leave 1/2 inch of headspace and seal the jars.
7. Place the jars in the prepared water bath canner and process for 10 minutes.

Apple and Lemon Jam with Honey

Yields: 6 half-pint jars

Ingredients:

- 3 cups sugar, granulated
- 6 cups apples, peeled, chopped, cored
- 1/2 cup honey
- Juice 4 lemons
- Zest of 4 lemons, grated

Directions:

1. Add lemon juice and apples into a non-reactive pot and let it simmer over medium heat.

2. Once the mixture begins to simmer, reduce the heat.

3. Allow the apples to cook until soft so you can mash them. Stir frequently to prevent burning.

4. Once the apples are soft, mash them coarsely using a potato masher.

5. Add honey and sugar to the mixture and mix well. Increase the heat to medium-high and let it simmer.

6. Let the mixture cook for another 10 minutes.

7. Remove the pot from heat and add lemon zest.

8. Put dollops of jam into the jars, leaving a space of 1/4 inch on the top of the jar. After removing the bubbles, seal the jars.

9. Place the jars in the boiling water bath and boil for 10 minutes, adjusting for altitude if required.

Christmas Jam

Yields: 2 – 3 half-pint jars

Ingredients:

- 1 1/2 cups whole fresh cranberries, chopped into chunks
- 1 teaspoon grated orange zest
- 1/2 orange, peeled, separated into sections, deseeded, chopped into chunks
- 1 cup fresh or frozen strawberries, slightly thawed, sliced
- 1/8 teaspoon ground cinnamon
- 1 cup sugar divided
- 1/8 teaspoon ground cloves
- 1 teaspoon calcium water
- 1 teaspoon Pomona's pectin powder

Directions:

1. To make calcium water, Mix 1/4 teaspoon of calcium powder from the box of Pomona's pectin and 1/4 cup water in a small

jar. Fasten the lid and shake the jar constantly until well combined. You need to use only 1 teaspoon of calcium water. So the rest can be stored in the refrigerator, and you can use it to make another batch of jelly or jam.

2. Add oranges, cranberries, orange zest, and strawberries into a food mill and strain the mixture. You can also blend them in a food processor.

3. Add the fruits, cinnamon, and cloves into a saucepan and place the saucepan over low heat. Stir constantly and cook for about 2 minutes.

4. Meanwhile, mix pectin powder and 1/2 cup sugar in a bowl.

5. When the fruit mixture starts boiling, stir in the pectin mixture. Stir constantly for a couple of minutes. When pectin dissolves completely, add the remaining sugar and keep stirring until the sugar dissolves.

6. When the mixture comes to a rapid boil, turn off the heat. Discard any scum that may be on the surface of the mixture every few minutes.

7. Spoon the jam into the prepared jars, leaving 1/4 inch of empty space on top of the jars. Remove the bubbles before sealing the jars.

8. Put the jars in the boiling water bath and process for 10 minutes. Adjust the timing for higher altitudes if necessary.

Cranberry and Pear Jam

Yields: 3 half-pint jars

Ingredients:

- 1 1/2 cups peeled, cored, crushed, fully ripe pears
- 1/8 cup unsweetened apple juice
- 2 3/4 cups granulated sugar
- 2.9 ounces liquid pectin

- 1/3 cup coarsely chopped dried cranberries
- 1/8 cup lemon juice
- 1/2 teaspoon ground cinnamon
- 1/4 teaspoon butter (optional but recommended to reduce foaming)

Directions:

1. Add pears, apple juice, cranberries, sugar, lemon juice, and butter, if using, into a saucepan.
2. Place the saucepan over high heat. When the mixture comes to a rapid boil, stir in pectin.
3. Let it boil rapidly for exactly 1 minute. Stir all the time. Turn off the heat. Discard any scum that may be on the surface of the mixture every few minutes.
4. Ladle the jam into the hot jars. Don't forget to leave a headspace of 1/4 inch. Remove the bubbles. Seal the jars.
5. Place the jars in the water bath canner for 10 minutes. Adjust for altitude if required.

Whole Strawberry Jam

Yields: 4 half-pint jars

Ingredients:

- 1.1 pounds small whole strawberries, hulled
- 1/4 bottle Certo liquid pectin
- 1 1/2 tablespoons lemon juice
- 1 1/2 pounds granulated sugar
- 1/4 teaspoon butter (optional but recommended to reduce foaming)

Directions:

1. Add strawberries, sugar, and lemon juice into a saucepan and

stir well. Set aside for an hour.

2. Add sugar and butter. Place the saucepan over high heat. Keep stirring continuously until it starts boiling rapidly. Let it boil rapidly for 2 1/2 - 3 minutes.

3. Discard any scum that may be floating on top. Add pectin and stir until well combined. Let the jam rest for about 15 – 17 minutes.

4. Spoon the jam into the jars. Make sure to leave a space of 1/4 inch on top of the jars, removing bubbles.

5. Process the jars in the prepared canner for 10 minutes. Adjust for altitude if required.

Raspberry and Redcurrant Jam

Yields: 4 – 5 half-pint jars

Ingredients:

- 8.8 ounces raspberries
- 23.8 ounces of granulated sugar
- 12 ounces red currants
- 1/4 bottle Certo liquid pectin

Directions:

1. Place red currants in a saucepan. Crush them with a potato masher.

2. Pour 2 1/2 tablespoons of water and place the pot over high heat.

3. When the mixture starts boiling, turn down the heat and cook covered for about 8 – 9 minutes.

4. Turn off the heat. Strain the currants in a food mill. Keep the strained currants aside and discard the seeds.

5. Place raspberries in a bowl and crush them with a potato masher. Now combine the currants and berries and weigh

them. You need 1.1 pounds of the fruit mixture. If it doesn't weigh to be 1.1 pounds, add enough water to make 1.1 pounds.

6. Add the fruit mixture into the saucepan. Place the saucepan over low heat.

7. Add sugar and often stir until sugar dissolves completely. Turn the heat to high and let it come to a rapid boil. Stir constantly for 3 minutes and turn off the heat.

8. Add pectin and stir. Let the jam cool for 2 – 3 minutes.

9. Spoon the jam into the jars. Make sure to leave a headspace of 1/4 inch, removing bubbles.

10. Process the jars in the prepared canner for 10 minutes. Adjust for altitude if required.

Caramel Apple Jam

Yields: 2 – 3 half-pint jars

Ingredients:

- 2 cups peeled, cored, diced sweet apples
- 1 cup peeled, cored, diced tart apples
- 1/2 package of powdered fruit pectin
- 3/4 cup light brown sugar
- 1 cup cane sugar
- 1/4 cup water
- 1/8 teaspoon ground nutmeg
- 1/4 teaspoon ground cinnamon

Directions:

1. Add apples and water into a Dutch oven or a heavy pot. Place the pot over low heat. Cook until the apples are tender and soft.

2. Add pectin and turn up the heat to high heat. Keep stirring until it starts boiling rapidly.

3. Mash the apple pieces that look uncooked with a potato masher.

4. Add spices, cane sugar, and brown sugar and constantly stir until the mixture quickly boils. Let it boil rapidly for exactly 1 minute, continually stirring. Turn off the heat.

5. Spoon the jam into the jars, leaving a space of 1/4 inch from the top of the jar. After removing the bubbles, seal the jars.

6. Put the jars in the boiling water bath and boil for 10 minutes, adjusting for altitude if required.

Water Bath Canning Marmalade Recipes

Blood Orange and Cardamom Marmalade

Yields: 6 half-pint jars

Ingredients:

- 6 pounds of blood oranges
- 1-quart water
- 25 – 30 pods of green cardamom
- 3 cups sugar or as required

Directions:

1. Take a sharp knife and cut a thin slice from the stem and bottom sides of the oranges and lemons so they can stand upright.
2. Carefully remove the peel from the oranges, ensuring you don't get any pith. You only need the peel, not the white pith, so use a sharp knife.
3. Chop the peel into thin, 1-inch strips. You can have slightly broader strips if you like chunky marmalade. Add the orange peels into a Dutch oven or pot. Pour water into the pot.
4. Roast the cardamom pods in a dry pan over medium-low heat for a few minutes until you get a nice aroma. Keep stirring the cardamom to prevent burning. Turn off the heat. Let the pods cool.
5. Remove all the pith surrounding the oranges.
6. Chop the fruit pulp and keep it aside for now.
7. Crush the cardamom pods lightly so that they split open. Place the pods in a tea ball or tie it up in cheesecloth.
8. Drop the tea ball in the pot with orange peels.
9. Place the pot over high heat. Let it cook uncovered for 20 – 30 minutes or until the peels of the oranges are soft. If the water gets absorbed and the mixture gets stuck to the bottom, add some water and cook until the peels are softened.
10. Add the oranges to the pot along with sugar. Increase the heat to medium heat and stir until the sugar dissolves completely.

Stir often for about 20 minutes. Remove any scum that may float on top whenever it is visible.

11. Place 1 – 2 plates in the refrigerator.

12. Let the mixture slowly come to 218 - 220 degrees F. Let it cook for 5 minutes at this temperature without stirring. Make sure the temperature does not go beyond this. The mixture is not to be stirred during these 5 minutes. Turn off the heat.

13. Take out the chilled plates from the refrigerator and drop some mixture (about a teaspoonful) on a plate. Now tilt the plate so that the marmalade spreads. Now take a spoon and move it through the marmalade.

14. The spoon will leave a line behind as you move it around. The plate will also be visible in part you moved the spoon around. Also, you may see wrinkles on the slightly cooled marmalade. If this happens, the marmalade is ready, or cook it for two more minutes.

15. Let the marmalade rest for 10 minutes. Take out the tea ball.

16. Spoon the marmalade into the hot jars. Make sure to leave 1/4 inch of empty space on top of the jars. Make sure all the jars have orange peels in them. Remove the bubbles before sealing the jars.

17. Process the jars in the prepared canner for 10 minutes. Adjust for altitude if required.

☆ ☆ ☆ ☆ ☆

Red Onion Marmalade

Yields: 2 – 3 half-pint jars

Ingredients:

- 3/4 cup thinly sliced red onions
- 1/8 cup lightly packed brown sugar
- 1 teaspoon grated orange zest
- 1/2 package (from a 2 ounces package) BERNARDIN

Original fruit pectin

- 1/4 cup finely chopped dried cranberries
- 1/8 cup cider vinegar
- 1 1/2 cups unsweetened apple juice
- 2 cups sugar
- 1/4 teaspoon butter (optional but recommended to reduce foaming)

Directions:

1. Add onions, brown sugar, cranberries, and vinegar to a heavy pan. Add butter if using, and place the pan over medium heat.
2. Stir often and cook until the onion is softened. Transfer the mixture to a stainless steel saucepan.
3. Add apple juice, orange zest, and pectin. Whisk until pectin dissolves and place the saucepan over high heat. Stir all the time.
4. Stir in the sugar. Keep stirring and let it come to a rapid boil. Now boil rapidly for a minute. Turn off the heat.
5. Spoon the jam into the jars, leaving a space of 1/4 inch from the top of the jar. Seal the jars after removing the bubbles.
6. Put the jars in the water bath canner and boil for 10 minutes. Adjust the time for higher altitudes.

Ground Cherry Marmalade

Yields: 3 – 4 half-pint jars

Ingredients:

- 1 1/2 cups stemmed, pitted, ground cherries
- 6 tablespoons water
- 2 tablespoons bottled lemon juice
- 1/2 pouch of liquid fruit pectin
- 1 cup cooked pears, drained, diced

- 1/4 cup drained, crushed, canned pineapple
- 3 1/2 cups sugar

Directions:

1. Add ground cherries, water, and pears into a pot. Cook the mixture over high heat.
2. When the mixture begins to boil, bring the heat to low and boil gently for about 20 minutes.
3. Stir in the sugar, lemon juice, and pineapple and continue stirring until the sugar dissolves. Allow it to come to a hard boil.
4. Stir in the pectin. Let it boil hard for 3 minutes. Turn off the heat.
5. Spoon the jam into the jars, leaving space of 1/4 inch from the top of the jar, removing bubbles. Now seal the jars.
6. Place the jars in the boiling water bath and boil for 10 minutes, adjusting for altitude if required.

Chili Orange Marmalade

Yields: 4 half-pint jars

Ingredients:

- 1 1/8 pounds ripe oranges, rinsed, dried, thinly sliced along with the peel, deseeded
- 4 1/2 cups granulated sugar
- 3 cups water
- 1 1/2 dried habanero chili peppers or 3 dried Colorado chili peppers, or 3 dried New Mexico chili peppers, cut into large pieces
- Zest of 1/2 lemon, grated
- Juice of 1/2 lemon, grated
- 1/4 teaspoon butter (optional but recommended)

Directions:

1. Add lemon zest, chopped oranges, water, and lemon juice into a heavy pot.
2. Place the pot over medium-high heat and let the mixture start boiling. Keep stirring until the sugar melts. Bring the mixture to a boil.
3. Boil gently on low heat for about 30 minutes. Stir on and off.
4. Place 1 – 2 plates in the freezer.
5. Drop the chili peppers into the pot and stir. Continue cooking for another 20 – 25 minutes or until the oranges are very soft.
6. Now, pick out the chili peppers and throw them off.
7. Add sugar and butter and stir.
8. Let the mixture slowly come to 220 degrees F. Let it cook for 5 minutes at this temperature without stirring. Make sure the temperature does not go beyond this. The mixture is not to be stirred during these 5 minutes. Remove any scum that may float on top.
9. Take out the chilled plates from the freezer and drop some marmalade (about a teaspoonful) on a plate. Now tilt the plate so that the marmalade spreads. Now take a spoon and move it through the marmalade.
10. The spoon will leave a line behind as you move it around. The plate will also be visible in part you moved the spoon around. Also, you may see wrinkles on the slightly cooled marmalade. If this happens, the marmalade is ready, or cook it for a couple of minutes longer.
11. Turn off the heat.
12. Fill the marmalade into the jars. Leaving a headspace of 1/4 inch is necessary. Remove the bubbles. Seal the jars.
13. Process the jars in the boiling water bath for 10 minutes. Adjust the timing for higher altitudes if required.

Lemon Marmalade

Yields: 2 – 3 half-pint jars

Ingredients:

- 1 pound lemons
- 3 1/2 cups water + extra for the peels
- 1/4 teaspoon baking soda, divided
- 2 cups sugar
- 1 drop of yellow food coloring (optional)

Directions:

1. Cut 1/4-inch thick slices from the stem side and bottom of the lemons so they can stand on the bottoms.
2. Carefully remove all the peel from the lemon with a sharp knife without the pith. Chop the peel into 1/4-inch thin strips.
3. Add the peels into a small saucepan.
4. Pour enough water over the peels so that they are just covered.
5. Add half the baking soda and place the saucepan over medium-high heat.
6. When it starts boiling, turn down the heat to medium-low heat. Cover the saucepan and cook for 8 – 10 minutes.
7. Drain off the water.
8. Carry out steps 4 – 7 once again.
9. Remove all the pith surrounding the citrus fruits and discard.
10. Cut the lemon segments lengthwise with a sharp knife and add to a bowl. Remove any loose membranes. Don't worry about the membranes that do not come off. Squeeze the membranes to remove any juice into a bowl.
11. Add lemon peel, lemon juice, lemon segments, and 3 1/2 cups of water into a pot. Place the pot over high heat.
12. When the mixture starts boiling, turn the heat to low and let it boil gently for about 20 minutes.
13. Stir in the sugar. Turn up the heat to medium heat. Stir occasionally. When the mixture starts boiling, turn down the

heat and cook for about 30 minutes or until slightly thick.

14. Turn off the heat. Add food coloring if using and stir well.

15. Ladle the marmalade into the hot jars. Leave 1/4 inch of empty space at the rim of the jars. Make sure all the jars have lemon peels. Debubble before sealing the jars.

16. Place the jars in the boiling water bath and process for 10 minutes, adjusting for altitude if required.

Strawberry Lemon Marmalade

Yields: 3 half-pint jars

Ingredients:

- 1/8 cup of very thin lemon slices (like paper)
- 2 cups hulled, crushed strawberries
- 3 cups granulated sugar
- 1/2 tablespoon lemon juice
- 1/2 package (from a 2 ounces package) BERNARDIN Original fruit pectin
- 1/4 teaspoon butter (optional but recommended to reduce foaming)

Directions:

1. Place lemon peel in a stainless steel saucepan, and add just enough water that they are covered.

2. Place the saucepan over medium heat. Cook covered until the peel turns soft. Drain off the cooked lemon peel water.

3. Now add lemon juice and strawberries into the saucepan with peel. Stir until well combined.

4. Add pectin and stir until pectin dissolves completely.

5. Now place the saucepan over high heat, stir it constantly and allow it to boil.

6. Stir in the sugar and butter if using.

7. Let it boil hard for 3 minutes. Turn off the heat. Remove any foam that may be on the surface of the jam.

8. Fill the jam into the jars. Leave 1/4 inch of headspace from the top of the jars, removing bubbles. Make sure to seal the jars finger-tight.

9. Place the jars in the water bath canner and boil for 10 minutes, adjusting for altitude if required.

Water Bath Canning Preserve Recipes

Figs Preserve

Yields: 5 half-pint jars

Ingredients:

- 1 1/2 quarts fresh whole figs
- 2 cups sugar
- 1 lemon, thinly sliced (optional)
- 6 cups boiling water
- 3 cups water

Directions:

1. Place figs in a pot. Pour boiling water over the figs. Let the figs soak in the boiling water for 15 minutes. Drain the figs in a colander. Rinse well with cold water and drain once again in the colander.
2. Combine sugar, lemon slices if using, and 3 cups of water in a pot and place the pot over medium heat. Stir often until the sugar dissolves completely. Let it boil hard for about 10 minutes. Remove any scum that may be found on the top of the syrup.
3. Add figs into the syrup and let it boil until the figs look sort of colorless. Remove figs with a slotted spoon and place in a pan. Continue cooking the syrup until it turns thick and resembles honey. Turn off the heat and transfer the syrup into the pan of figs.
4. Transfer the pan to the refrigerator when the syrup and figs cool completely.
5. Now take it out of the refrigerator and place it over high heat. When the syrup starts boiling, turn off the heat. Remove figs with a slotted spoon and place them in the jars.
6. Fill up the jars with syrup leaving 1/4 inch of space at the top. Remove the bubbles before sealing the jars.
7. Process the jars in the water bath canner for 5 minutes. Adjust for altitude if required.

Ground Cherry Preserves

Yields: 4 half-pint jars

Ingredients:

- 3 cups stemmed, pitted, ground cherries
- 4 cups sugar
- 3/4 cup light corn syrup
- 1/2 cup water
- 2 tablespoons bottled lemon juice

Directions:

1. Add water and cherries into a pot and place the pot over high heat.
2. Stir often and let it come to a boil. Bring down the heat to low and boil gently for about 6 – 7 minutes. Stirring on and off.
3. Stir in the sugar, corn syrup, and lemon juice. Turn up the heat to high heat. Stir often. When the mixture starts boiling again, turn down the heat and cook for about 20 – 25 minutes. Turn off the heat and cool for 7 – 8 hours.
4. Heat the mixture to boiling point and turn off the heat.
5. Spoon the preserves into the jars, leaving a space of 1/4 inch from the top of the jar. Removing bubbles before sealing the jars is a must.
6. Put the jars in the boiling water bath and boil for 10 minutes, adjusting the time for higher altitudes if required.

Kiwi Preserves

Yields: 6 half-pint jars

Ingredients:

- 8 kiwifruits, peeled, thinly sliced
- 6 tablespoons unsweetened pineapple juice
- 1/2 pouch (from a 2.9 ounces pouch) of liquid pectin
- 1 1/2 cups granulated sugar
- 2 tablespoons lime juice
- 1/4 teaspoon butter (optional but recommended to reduce foaming)

Directions:

1. Add sugar, lime juice, kiwifruit, pineapple juice, and butter into a stainless steel saucepan.
2. Place the saucepan over high heat. Stir all the time until it comes to a hard boil that you cannot stir down.
3. Add pectin and stir. Let it come to a boil once again and boil rapidly for exactly 1 minute while stirring. Remove the saucepan from the heat. Discard any scum that may be on the surface.
4. Fill the mixture into the jars. Make sure to leave space of 1/4 inch on the top of the jars, removing bubbles. Make sure to seal the jars.
5. Put the jars in the water bath canner and process for 10 minutes. Change the timing for higher altitudes if required.

Spiced Cherry Preserves

Yields: 4-pint jars

Ingredients:

- 6 pounds cherries, rinsed, stemmed, pitted

- 2 cups water
- 2 teaspoons small cinnamon stick pieces
- 2 teaspoons black peppercorns
- 2 cups sugar
- Juice of 2 lemons
- Zest of 2 lemons, grated
- 2 teaspoons whole cloves
- 6-star anise

Directions:

1. Add water, sugar, lemon juice, and zest into a saucepan.
2. Combine the spices in a tea ball or tie them up in cheesecloth. Drop the tea ball into the pot.
3. Put the saucepan over high heat. Stir often until the sugar dissolves. When the syrup starts boiling, mix the cherries into the syrup. When the mixture starts boiling again, turn the heat to medium-high heat and simmer until the cherries are cooked. Turn off the heat. Pick out the tea ball and discard the spices.
4. Remove cherries using a slotted spoon and place them in the jars.
5. Pour syrup to fill up the jars leaving 1/4 inch of empty space on the neck of the jars. Make sure to remove the bubbles before sealing the jars.
6. Place the jars in the boiling water bath and boil for 15 minutes. Adjust for altitude if required.

Watermelon Rind Preserves

Yields: 3 half-pint jars

Ingredients:

- 3/4 quart trimmed, peeled, cut watermelon rind pieces
- 1 quart water + 3 1/2 cups water extra water for covering and

cooking

- 2 cups sugar
- 3 1/2 cups water
- 2 tablespoons salt
- 1/2 tablespoon ground ginger
- 2 tablespoons lemon juice
- 1/2 lemon, thinly sliced (optional)

Directions:

1. You only need the rind of the watermelon and not the fruit or peel. Chop them into about 1-inch cubes.
2. Combine the salt and 1 quart of water in a container. Add the rind pieces and place the container in the refrigerator for about 6 hours.
3. Drain in a colander. Rinse well and drain in a colander. Add the rind pieces into the container. Pour enough water to cover the rind pieces. Let the rinds soak for 30 minutes.
4. Drain well. Transfer the rinds into a pot. Add ginger to the pot. Pour enough water to cover the rinds. Place the pot over high heat. Cook until the rinds are soft and can be pierced with a fork. Drain the rinds in a colander.
5. Add lemon juice, sugar, and 3 1/2 cups of water into the pot. Place the pot over high heat. When the syrup starts boiling, allow it to boil rapidly for 5 minutes.
6. Add the rinds and turn down the heat. Cook for about 20 minutes, and stir in the lemon slices if using. Cook until the rind pieces are translucent. Turn off the heat.
7. Spoon the mixture into the jars, leaving space of 1/4 inch from the top of the jar, removing bubbles.
8. The jars are to be processed in the water bath canner for 5 minutes. Change the timing for higher altitudes if required.

Cranberry Salad with Pineapple and Oranges

Yields: 4 – 5 half-pint jars

Ingredients:

- 3/4 cup chopped fresh cranberries
- 1/2 small can (from an 11 ounce can) of mandarin oranges
- 1 cup sugar divided
- 3 tablespoons ClearJel mixed with 3 tablespoons pineapple juice from the can or extra cranberry juice
- 1/2 large can (from a 20-ounce can) of crushed pineapple or tidbits, drained but retaining the liquid
- 2 tablespoons bottled lemon juice
- 3/4 cup cranberry juice, divided
- 1/2 cup chopped walnuts or pecans (optional)

Directions:

1. Combine 1/4 cup sugar and 1/4 cup cranberry juice in a saucepan over medium heat.
2. When the mixture starts boiling, stir in the oranges, pineapples, remaining cranberry juice, lemon juice, and most of the sugar.
3. Stir often until the mixture starts boiling.
4. In the meantime, mix the remaining sugar, ClearJel, and pineapple juice in a cup.
5. Pour the ClearJel mixture into the pot, constantly stirring while adding. Keep stirring until slightly thick.
6. Turn off the heat. Add walnuts if using. Turn off the heat.
7. Spoon the mixture into the jars, leaving a space of 1/2 inch from the top of the jar. Seal the jars after removing the bubbles.
8. The jars are to be placed in the prepared canner and processed for 10 minutes. Adjust the timing for higher altitudes.

★ ★ ★ ★ ★

Fruit Salad

Yields: 7 – 8 pint jars

Ingredients:

- 2 1/2 cups sugar
- 1 pound plums, pitted, cut into 1/2 inch pieces
- 1 pound pears, peeled, cored, cut into 1/2 inch pieces
- 1 pound big cherries, halved, pitted
- 1/2 pineapple, peeled, cored, cut into tidbits
- 1 pound apricots, pitted, cut into 1/2 inch cubes
- 1 pound apples, cored, cut into 1/2 inch cubes
- 1 pound grapes
- 1 pound peaches
- 4 cups water + extra for peaches
- 1 cup pineapple juice, unsweetened

Directions:

1. To prepare the peaches: Have a bowl of cold water on your countertop.
2. Boil a pot of water over high heat. When water starts boiling, Drop peaches in the boiling water. Drain off after 30 – 60 seconds and not longer than 60 seconds. This process makes peeling easier.
3. Drain the peaches in a colander and immediately drop the peaches in the bowl of cold water. This stops further cooking. When the peaches are cooled, peel the skin of the peaches. Discard the skin.
4. Prepare the lemon water by adding about 2 teaspoons of lemon juice to a bowl half filled with water.
5. Cut the peaches into 1/2 - 1 inch pieces. As you chop the fruit, drop them into the bowl of lemon water. This prevents the

browning of fruits, especially pears, peaches, and apples.

6. Add grapes, pears, apricots, pineapple, plum, apples, and cherries into the bowl of lemon water.

7. Add pineapple juice, sugar, and water into a saucepan.

8. Place the saucepan over medium heat. Stir constantly until the sugar dissolves completely. When the syrup starts boiling, turn off the heat.

9. Drain the fruits from the bowl of lemon water just before filling the jars. Place the fruits in the jars. Divide the fruits equally among the jars.

10. Pour syrup to fill up the jars leaving 1/2 inch headspace. Remove the bubbles before sealing the jars.

11. Place the jars in the boiling water bath and process for 15 minutes. Adjust for altitude if required.

Water Bath Canning Slaw, Chow Chow, etc. Recipes

Red Cabbage Slaw

Yields: 2 – 3 pint jars

Ingredients:

- 3 pounds red cabbage, rinsed well, remove the outermost leaves, shredded or grated
- 1/4 cup sugar
- 1 tablespoon mustard seeds
- 1 tablespoon allspice berries
- 2 cups red wine vinegar (5% acidity)
- 2 tablespoons pickling and preserving salt
- 1 stick cinnamon, broken into pieces
- 1 tablespoon caraway seeds
- 1 tablespoon black peppercorns
- Pickle crisp (optional)

Directions:

1. Place a layer of cabbage in a bowl.
2. Sprinkle some pickling salt over the cabbage. Repeat these layers until all the cabbage and salt are used up.
3. Cover the bowl and put the bowl in the refrigerator for 24 hours.
4. Take out the bowl of cabbage and rinse well. Drain well in a colander.
5. Take about 2 baking sheets and line them with paper towels. Spread the cabbage on the baking sheets.
6. Tie up the spices in cheesecloth and add to a saucepan. Add sugar and vinegar and place the saucepan over medium heat. Allow it to boil for 5 minutes, and turn off the heat. Pick out the spice bag and discard it.
7. Fill the prepared jars with cabbage. Leave 1/2 inch of space from the top of the jars.
8. Pour the vinegar solution into the jars and leave 1/2 inch space from the top, removing bubbles.

9. Sprinkle pickle crisp in each jar if using. Seal the jars.

10. Put the jars in the water bath canner and process for 20 minutes. Adjust for altitude if required.

Chayote and Jicama Slaw

Yields: 3 half-pint jars

Ingredients:

- 2 cups julienne cut jicama
- 1 cup finely chopped red bell pepper
- 2 cups julienne cut chayote
- 1 hot pepper, finely chopped
- 11/4 cups cider vinegar (5% acidity)
- 1/2 teaspoon celery seeds (optional)
- 1 3/4 teaspoon canning salt
- 1 1/4 cups water
- 1/4 cup white sugar

Directions:

1. Add jicama, bell pepper, hot pepper, vinegar, celery seeds, canning salt, water, and sugar into a Dutch oven or heavy pot. Place the pot over high heat.

2. Allow it to boil for 5 minutes. Turn the heat to low and stir in the chayote. When it starts boiling once again, remove it from the heat.

3. Remove the vegetables using a slotted spoon and put them in the jars. Leave ½ inch of space on the top of the jars. Pour the hot liquid into the jars, making sure to maintain 1/2 inch space on top. Seal the jars after removing bubbles.

4. The jars are to be ped in the boiling water bath for 15 minutes. Adjust the time if you live in higher altitudes.

Coleslaw

Yields: 6 half-pint jars

Ingredients:

- 1 pound cabbage, shredded
- 1 1/2 large carrots, peeled, shredded
- 1/2 large green bell pepper, thinly sliced
- 1/2 teaspoon salt
- 1/2 cup chopped onions

For the syrup:

- 1/2 teaspoon celery seeds
- 1/2 teaspoon mustard seeds
- 1 cup sugar or as per your taste
- 1/2 cup vinegar (5% acidity)
- 1/4 cup water

Directions:

1. Combine the vegetables and salt in a colander. Let it drain for an hour.
2. To make syrup: Add mustard, celery, vinegar, water, and sugar into a pot and place the pot over high heat. When the mixture starts boiling, allow it to boil for 3 minutes.
3. Turn off the heat and let the solution cool. Place the cabbage mixture in a bowl. Add the solution to the bowl of cabbage. After 5 minutes, give it a good stir.
4. Remove the vegetables from the bowl using a slotted spoon and place them in the jars. Leave 1 inch of space from the top of the jars.
5. Pour the solution from the bowl of cabbage into the jars. Don't forget to leave 1/2 inch space on top, removing bubbles. Seal

the jars.

6. Process the jars in the prepared canner for 15 minutes. Adjust for altitude if required.

Green Tomato Chow Chow

Yields: 4 – 5 pint jars

Ingredients:

- 5 pounds green tomatoes
- 6 green bell peppers
- 3 hot peppers, chopped
- 4 large onions, peeled
- 1 1/2 tablespoons salt
- 2 cups white vinegar
- 4 – 6 whole cloves
- 3 – 4 bay leaves
- 1 1/2 tablespoons dry mustard
- 1/4 cup horseradish (optional)
- 1/2 tablespoon allspice berries
- 1 1/2 tablespoons dry mustard powder

Directions:

1. You can chop the onions, tomatoes, and bell peppers or grind them. Place them in a nonreactive bowl. Sprinkle salt over the ingredients and mix well.
2. Keep the bowl covered in the refrigerator for 6 – 8 hours.
3. Drain the mixture well and add into a saucepan. Tie up the spices in cheesecloth or put them in a tea bag and drop them into the saucepan. Add vinegar, mustard, and sugar and stir.
4. Cook the mixture over medium heat. Stir often until the sugar dissolves completely. Cook until the vegetables are tender. Turn off the heat.

5. Stir in horseradish. Spoon the mixture into the prepared jars. Make sure to leave 1/2 inch space on top, removing bubbles. Seal the jars.

6. The jars are to be processed in the water bath canner for 10 minutes. Adjust for altitude if required.

Cabbage and Cauliflower Chow Chow

Yields: 3-pint jars

Ingredients:

- 1/2 quart chopped cabbage
- 1 cup chopped green tomatoes
- 1 cup chopped green bell pepper
- 1 1/2 cups chopped cauliflower
- 1 cup chopped onion
- 1/2 cup chopped red bell pepper
- 1 1/2 tablespoons salt
- 1 1/4 cups vinegar
- 1 teaspoon celery seeds
- 1/2 teaspoon mustard seeds
- 3/4 cup sugar
- 1 teaspoon dry mustard powder
- 1/4 teaspoon ground ginger
- 1/2 teaspoon turmeric powder

Directions:

1. Place the vegetables in a nonreactive bowl. Sprinkle salt over the ingredients and mix well.
2. Keep the bowl covered in the refrigerator for 4 – 6 hours.
3. Drain the mixture. Rinse well and drain well.
4. Combine the vinegar, celery seeds, mustard seeds, sugar, mustard, ginger, and turmeric in a saucepan. Place the

saucepan over medium heat, and cook for about 10 minutes, stirring often until the sugar dissolves.

5. Add the vegetables and mix well. Cook for about 10 minutes. Turn off the heat.

6. Spoon the mixture into the prepared jars. Make sure to leave 1/2 inch of space on top. After removing the bubbles, seal the jars.

7. Put the jars in the boiling water bath and boil for 10 minutes, adjusting the timing for higher altitude.

Cucumber and Cabbage Chow Chow

Yields: 6 pints

Ingredients:

- 2 small green cabbages, grated
- 2 medium onions, diced
- 2 medium cucumbers, peeled, finely chopped
- 2 red bell peppers, diced
- 2 cups apple cider vinegar
- 1 cup water
- 2 teaspoons celery seeds
- 1 1/3 cups light brown sugar, packed
- 4 teaspoons dry mustard powder
- 2 teaspoons turmeric powder

Directions:

1. Place the cabbage, onions, cucumbers, and bell peppers in a nonreactive bowl. Sprinkle salt over the vegetables and mix well.

2. Keep the bowl covered loosely with a kitchen towel on your countertop for 8 – 10 hours.

3. Drain the mixture in a colander. Press well to remove any moisture from the vegetables.

4. In a saucepan, combine vinegar, celery seeds, brown sugar, water, mustard, and turmeric. Place the saucepan over medium heat, and cook for about 10 minutes, stirring until the sugar dissolves.

5. Add the vegetables and mix well. Cook for about 15 minutes. Turn off the heat.

6. Spoon the mixture into the prepared jars. Do not forget to leave 1/2 inch of space on top. Seal the jars after removing the bubbles.

7. The jars are to be processed in the water bath canner for 10 minutes, adjusting for altitude if required.

Dessert Sauce Recipes

Cranberry Sauce

Yields: 6 half-pint size jars

Ingredients:

- 2 pounds fresh or frozen cranberries (thawed if using frozen cranberries)
- 1/2 cup unsweetened apple juice or extra orange juice
- 5 tablespoons apple cider vinegar
- 12 whole cloves
- 1 teaspoon red chili flakes
- 1/4 teaspoon pepper
- Juice Of 4 Oranges
- Zest Of 4 Oranges, Grated
- 1 3/4 cups granulated sugar
- 2-star anise
- 2 sticks cinnamon (2 inches each)
- 1/2 teaspoon fine sea salt or kosher salt or to taste

Directions:

1. Add sugar, apple juice, spices, salt, orange juice, and orange zest into a pot and stir.
2. Cook the mixture over high heat, stirring until it starts boiling. Bring the heat to medium heat and cook for about 10 minutes. Stir often.
3. Add cranberries into the pot and give it a good stir.
4. Keep the pot covered, leaving it very partially open. Soon you will hear the mild sound of the berries popping. Uncover and cook for 10 minutes when the popping sound stops. Make sure you stir it often.
5. Taste a bit of the sauce and add more salt and chili flakes if desired.
6. Ladle the sauce into the jars leaving 3/4 inch headspace. Remove the bubbles. Seal the jars.

7. Place the jars in the water bath canner and process for 10 minutes. Adjust for altitude if required.

Chocolate Raspberry Sauce

Yields: 3 half-pint jars

Ingredients:

- 2 1/4 cups crushed red raspberries
- 3 tablespoons Ball Real Fruit pectin powder
- 3 1/2 cups white sugar or more to taste
- 1 ounce bottled lemon juice
- 4 tablespoons cocoa powder, sifted

Directions:

1. Depending on your preference, you can either mash the raspberries or crush them with a potato masher until smooth.
2. Add the raspberries and lemon juice to a pan. Sift the cocoa directly into a bowl. Add pectin. Mix well.
3. Place the saucepan over medium-high heat. Add the pectin mixture and keep stirring until the pectin dissolves completely.
4. When it starts boiling, stir in the sugar.
5. Turn the heat to medium. Let it boil rapidly for a minute. Remove any scum or foam that may float on top. Remove the pan from heat.
6. Ladle the sauce into the jars leaving 1/4 inch headspace. Seal the jars after removing the bubbles.
7. Immerse the jars in the boiling water bath and process for 10 minutes. Adjust the time for altitude.

Strawberry Sauce

Yields: 8 half-pint jars

Ingredients:

- 4.4 pounds strawberries, quartered or thickly sliced
- 4 teaspoons calcium water
- 1 teaspoon Pomona's pectin powder
- 2 cups sugar or 1 cup honey or 2 teaspoons liquid stevia

Directions:

1. To make calcium water, add 1/4 teaspoon of calcium powder (that comes in the box of Pomona's pectin) and 1/4 cup of water into a jar. Fasten the lid and shake the jar constantly until well incorporated. 4 teaspoons of calcium water is required to make the sauce. Place the remaining calcium water in the refrigerator, which can be used later to make another batch of jelly, jam, or sauce.

2. Mash the strawberries a little at a time and add them to a bowl. You can use a potato masher for mashing. Put the mashed strawberries into a bowl as you mash. Measure the strawberries. You need 8 cups of it.

3. Take out about 1/2 cup of the juice from the bowl of mashed strawberries.

4. Add the pectin powder to the juice and whisk well. Add the sweetener and whisk well. Keep it aside for now.

5. Add the strawberries and calcium water into a stainless steel pot. Place the pot over high heat. When the mixture starts boiling, add the pectin mixture a little each time while stirring continuously.

6. Let it boil hard for 2 minutes, stirring all the time. Turn off the heat.

7. Pour the sauce into jars, and let there be f 1/4 inch of empty space at the rim of the jars. After removing the bubbles, make sure to seal the jars.

8. Let the jars be placed in the water bath canner and processed for 10 minutes. Adjust for altitude if required.

Peach Rum Sauce

Yields: 3 – 4 half-pint jars

Ingredients:

- 3 cups chopped, pitted, peeled peaches
- 1 cup granulated sugar
- 1/2 teaspoon grated lemon zest
- 1 cup lightly packed brown sugar
- 6 tablespoons rum

Directions:

1. To prepare the peaches: Have a bowl of cold water on your countertop.
2. Boil a pot of water over high heat. When water starts boiling, Drop peaches in the boiling water. Drain off after 30 – 60 seconds and not longer than 60 seconds. This process makes peeling easier.
3. Drain the peaches in a colander and immediately drop the peaches in the bowl of cold water. This stops further cooking. When the peaches are cooled, peel the skin of the peaches. Discard the skin.
4. Make the lemon water by adding about 2 teaspoons of lemon juice to a bowl half filled with water.
5. Cut the peaches into 1/2 - 1 inch pieces. As you chop the peaches, drop them into the bowl of lemon water. This prevents the browning of the peaches.
6. Drain the peaches and add them into a stainless steel saucepan. Add rum, lemon zest, brown, and granulated sugar and place it over high heat.

7. Stir constantly. When it starts boiling, turn the heat to low. Cook until thick; stir on and off. Turn off the heat.

8. Pour the sauce into jars. Leave 1/4 inch of empty space at the neck of the jars. Seal the jars after you remove the bubbles.

9. The jars are to be submerged in the water bath canner and processed for 10 minutes.

10. Adjust for higher altitude if required.

Blueberry Lemon Dessert Sauce

Yields: 4-pint jars

Ingredients:

- 8 cups fresh blueberries, stemmed
- 2 teaspoons grated fresh lemon zest
- 2 pouches (3 ounces each) of Ball Liquid fruit pectin
- 6 cups granulated sugar
- 2 tablespoons fresh lemon juice

Directions:

1. Fill a large pot halfway through with water. Boil the water over high heat.

2. When water starts boiling, turn the heat to low.

3. In the meantime, add the blueberries into a Dutch oven or heavy-bottomed stainless steel pot. Crush the berries lightly with a potato masher, taking care not to mash them.

4. Mix the sugar, lemon juice, and lemon zest with the blueberries. Place the pot over high heat.

5. Keep stirring until it starts boiling. Let it come to a rapid boil.

6. Stir in pectin and keep stirring. Let it boil rapidly for 1 minute. Make sure you are stirring all the time. Turn off the heat. Remove the foam that may be seen on the surface of the mixture.

7. Turn off the heat.

8. Ladle the sauce into jars with a headspace of 1/4 inch. Debubble before sealing the jars.

9. Place the jars in the prepared boiling water bath and process for 10 minutes. Adjust the time for altitude.

Condiment Recipes

Blackberry Chipotle Glaze

Yields: 4 half-pint jars

Ingredients:

- 2 teaspoons olive oil
- 6 cloves garlic, chopped
- 18 ounces frozen blackberries, thawed, drained
- 1 cup sugar
- 2 cups diced onions
- 2 tablespoons chopped chipotle chilies in adobo sauce, deseeded
- 1 1/2 cups balsamic vinegar
- 2 teaspoons salt

Directions:

1. Pour oil into a saucepan and let it heat over medium-high heat. When the oil is hot, add onions and cook until translucent.
2. Stir in the garlic. Cook for about a minute or until you get a nice aroma.
3. Add chipotle chilies and keep stirring for about a minute. Stir in the sugar, blackberries, salt, and vinegar.
4. Stir often when the mixture starts boiling. Turn the heat to low and cook until it is about 3 cups. Turn off the heat.
5. Transfer the mixture to a food mill and strain the mixture. Place a wire mesh strainer over a bowl. Pour the mixture into the strainer and strain into the bowl. Discard the solids.
6. Pour the strained blackberries into the pot. Cook over medium heat for about 5 – 7 minutes.
7. Pour the glaze into jars. Debubble and make sure there is headspace of 1/4 inch before sealing the jars.
8. The jars are to be processed in the water bath canner for 15 minutes, adjusting for altitude if required.

Bourbon Brown Sugar Mustard

Yields: 6 half-pint jars

Ingredients:

- 2 cups bourbon
- 2 cups brown mustard seeds
- 12 tablespoons yellow mustard powder
- 2 teaspoons salt
- 1 cup filtered water
- 1 cup cider vinegar
- 1 cup lightly packed brown sugar

Directions:

1. Add mustard seeds, water, and bourbon into a small bowl and stir well. Let it soak for at least 4 hours and up to 9 hours.
2. Transfer the mixture to a saucepan. Place the saucepan over high heat. When it starts boiling, turn off the heat and let it soak for 2 hours.
3. Now grind the soaked mustard seeds with any soaking liquid until the desired texture is achieved.
4. Add sugar, salt, and mustard powder into a saucepan. Pour vinegar and mix well.
5. Place the saucepan over medium heat. Stir all the time until it starts boiling. Boil until thickened, as per your preference. Keep in mind that the sauce will thicken further on cooling. Stir on and off.
6. Turn off the heat.
7. Fill the sauce into jars. Leave empty space of 1/4 inch at the rim of the jars. Debubble and seal the jars.
8. Process the jars in the prepared canner for 15 minutes. Adjust for altitude if required.

Dijon Mustard

Yields: 3 – 4 half-pint size jars

Ingredients:

- 1 cup chopped onion
- 1/2 cup white wine vinegar with 5% acidity
- 3 medium cloves garlic, peeled, coarsely chopped
- 2 small sprigs of rosemary
- 3 tablespoons dry mustard
- 1 cup Pinot Grigio wine or any other dry white wine of your choice
- 1/2 teaspoon table salt
- 2 whole black peppercorns
- 1/2 cup yellow mustard seeds
- 1 1/3 cups water or as required

Directions:

1. Add rosemary sprigs, garlic, vinegar, onion, wine, salt, and peppercorns into a stainless steel saucepan.
2. Cook the mixture over high heat. When the mixture starts boiling, bring down the heat to low and cook until the onions are softened. Stir on and off.
3. Turn off the heat. Place a wire mesh strainer over a glass or stainless steel bowl. Strain the onion mixture through the strainer. The solids are no longer needed.
4. Add mustard seeds and dry mustard into the bowl of strained liquid. Keep the bowl covered at room temperature for 24 – 48 hours but no longer than 48 hours.
5. Grind the mustard mixture, adding water until nearly smooth but not completely smooth. It should resemble cooked oatmeal. You may not require all of the water. So, add water accordingly.
6. Add the mustard mixture into the saucepan and cook the mixture over medium-high heat until it begins to boil. Next let

it boil gently on low heat uncovered for about 4 – 5 minutes.

7. Ladle the sauce into the hot jars. Leave 1/4 inch of space on the top of the jars. Seal the jars after debubbling.

8. Immerse the jars in the boiling water bath and process for 15 minutes, adjusting for altitude if required.

Honey Mustard

Yields: 3 half-pint jars

Ingredients:

- 1 1/2 cups apple cider vinegar
- 1 cup honey
- 3 teaspoons white sugar
- 2/3 cup water
- 1 cup mustard powder

Directions:

1. Add vinegar, honey, sugar, water, and mustard powder to a pot. Place the pot over medium-high heat.

2. Stir often until the sugar dissolves. Cook uncovered until slightly thick. Remember, it will thicken on cooling.

3. Pour the sauce into the prepared jars. Leave 1/4 inch of empty space from the rim of the jars. Dissipate the air bubbles before sealing the jars.

4. Place the jars in the boiling water bath and process for 15 minutes, adjusting the time for higher altitude.

Cranberry Ketchup

Yields: 4 half-pint jars

Ingredients:

- 1 1/2 pounds cranberries, rinsed, stemmed
- 2 – 3 cloves garlic, peeled
- 1 cup chopped onion
- 3/4 cup water
- 1 teaspoon mustard powder
- 1/2 teaspoon salt
- 1/4 teaspoon ground allspice
- 1 1/2 cups lightly packed brown sugar
- 1/2 cup white vinegar
- 1/2 teaspoon ground cloves
- 1/2 teaspoon pepper
- 1/4 teaspoon cayenne pepper

Directions:

1. Add onion, cranberries, and garlic into a stainless steel pot and place it over high heat. Stir until it comes to a boil.
2. Turn the heat to low and cook until you can hear a mild popping sound from the cranberries.
3. When the popping stops, turn off the heat. Pass the mixture through a food mill.
4. Pour the strained mixture into the same pot. Add salt, spices, sugar, and vinegar and mix well.
5. Stir often until the sugar dissolves, and the mixture starts boiling. Turn the heat to low and cook until thick. Take a heaping spoonful of the mixture. If the heap remains as it is, without disintegrating, the ketchup is ready; if not, cook the mixture for some more time until it doesn't disintegrate.
6. Taste a bit of it. If it is not sweet enough, you can add a little stevia to taste. This is optional.

7. Spoon the ketchup into the prepared jars. Leave 1/2 inch of space from the top of the jars. De-bubble before sealing the jars.

8. Immerse the jars in the water bath canner and process for 15 minutes. Change the timing for higher altitudes.

Steak Sauce

Yields: 4 – 5 half-pint jars

Ingredients:

- 2 cups ketchup (preferably homemade)
- 2 large cloves garlic, peeled
- 1/2 cup Worcestershire sauce
- 1/2 cup white vinegar
- 4 tablespoons brown sugar
- 1 cup coarsely chopped onions
- 1/2 cup water
- 1/2 cup bottled lemon juice
- 4 tablespoons soy sauce
- 2 tablespoons prepared yellow mustard (preferably homemade)

Directions:

1. Add ketchup, garlic, Worcestershire sauce, vinegar, sugar, onions, water, lemon juice, soy sauce, and mustard into a saucepan.

2. Cook the mixture until it boils over medium heat. Turn the heat to low and simmer until the desired consistency is achieved.

3. Pass the mixture through a wire mesh strainer and strain the mixture into a bowl.

4. Discard the solids.

5. Fill the sauce in the jars. Leave 1/2 inch of empty space on top of the jars. Remove the bubbles before you seal the jars.

6. Submerge the jars in the boiling water bath for 15 minutes. Adjust for altitude if required.

Barbecue Sauce

Yields: 2 – 3 pint-size jars

Ingredients:

- 12 large tomatoes; remove any stems and leaves
- 1 cup chopped onion
- 1 hot red pepper, cored, chopped
- 1 clove garlic, crushed
- 1/2 tablespoon dry mustard
- 1/2 tablespoon canning salt
- Cayenne pepper to taste
- 1 cup chopped celery
- 3/4 cup chopped sweet red or green bell pepper
- 1/2 teaspoon black peppercorns
- 1/2 cup brown sugar
- 1/2 tablespoon paprika
- 1/2 teaspoon Tabasco sauce or any other hot pepper sauce
- 10 tablespoons 5% vinegar

Directions:

1. Boil a pot of water over high heat. While the water is boiling, make an 'X' on the bottom of each tomato using a paring knife.

2. Have a bowl of ice water ready on your countertop near the stovetop. Drop the tomatoes carefully into the pot of boiling water. Let the tomatoes cook for a minute. Soon you can see

a bit of loose skin around the area of the 'X' on the tomatoes.

3. Lift the tomatoes with a slotted spoon, one or two at a time, and drop them into the bowl of ice water. Let the tomatoes remain in this bowl for a while to cool.

4. Peel off the skin from the tomatoes over a bowl so that any juice while peeling can be collected.

5. Chop the peeled tomatoes.

6. Measure out 4 1/2 cups and add into a saucepan.

7. Add onion, celery, and peppers into the saucepan with the tomatoes and cook over medium heat until soft.

8. Pour the mixture into a food mill and strain the mixture. Discard the solids.

9. Pour the strained mixture into the saucepan. Place peppercorns on a piece of cheesecloth and tie it up. You can also put them in a tea ball if desired.

10. Drop the spice bag into the saucepan. Add brown sugar, paprika, vinegar, Tabasco sauce, and salt, and cook until the sauce is half its original quantity. Stir occasionally. Turn off the heat.

11. Discard the spice bag.

12. Pour sauce into the jars. Make sure to leave 1/2 inch of empty space on the top of the jars. Debubble and seal the jars.

13. The jars are to be processed in the prepared canner for 10 minutes. Adjust the time for altitude.

Seafood Cocktail Sauce

Yields: 4 – 5

Ingredients:

- 1/2 cups prepared tomatoes
- Juice of a lemon
- Zest of a lemon, grated

- 10 tablespoons granulated sugar
- 1 tablespoon pickling salt
- 1 teaspoon dry mustard
- 1/2 teaspoon onion powder
- 1 1/2 cups peeled, finely grated horseradish
- 2 cloves garlic, peeled, minced
- 1/2 cup white vinegar
- 1 tablespoon Worcestershire sauce
- 1/2 teaspoon cayenne pepper
- 1/4 teaspoon pepper

Directions:

1. To prepare the tomatoes, chop them into pieces and pass them through a food mill or a sieve. Pour the strained tomatoes into a large measuring cup and measure 6 1/2 cups.
2. Pour the strained tomatoes into a saucepan. Place the saucepan over medium-high heat.
3. When the tomatoes start boiling, turn the heat to low and simmer until it is half their original quantity, i.e., about 3 1/4 cups.
4. Combine the lemon peel, sugar, Worcestershire sauce, lemon zest, sugar, salt, and spices with the tomatoes in the saucepan.
5. Stir often. When the mixture starts boiling, turn off the heat. Add horseradish and stir.
6. Ladle the sauce into the jars leaving 1/2 inch of space from the top. Remove the bubbles before sealing the jars.
7. Place the jars in the boiling water bath and process for 10 minutes. Adjust for higher altitude if required.

Cayenne Pepper Sauce

Yields: 2 – 3 pint-size jars

Ingredients:

- 1 1/2 pound Anaheim or Hungarian or jalapeño peppers
- 2 cups sliced onion
- 1 1/2 cans (28 ounces each) of diced tomatoes with their liquid
- 1 1/4 cups water
- 3 tablespoons minced garlic
- 3 tablespoons chopped cilantro
- 1 1/2 cups 5% cider vinegar

Directions:

1. Add onion, peppers, water, garlic, cilantro, and vinegar into a stock pot. Place the pot over medium heat.
2. Cook covered for about 40 – 50 minutes. Stir on and off.
3. Reduce the heat to low and cook for about 45 – 50 minutes. Turn off the heat.
4. Pass the mixture through a food mill and strain the sauce. Blending the mixture in a blender is a better idea.
5. Fill sauce into the jars having 1/4 inch headspace at the top and remove the bubbles. Seal the jars.
6. Place the jars in the water bath canner and process for 10 minutes. Adjust the time for higher altitudes.

★ ★ ★ ★ ★

Chicken Wing Sauce

Yields: 4 half-pint jars

Ingredients:

- 2 1/2 pounds tomatoes
- 3 tablespoons brown sugar

- 3/4 cup white vinegar
- 1 clove garlic, peeled, minced
- 1/2 teaspoon ground ginger or to taste
- 1 cup chopped onion
- 1/4 teaspoon cayenne pepper
- 2 teaspoons pickling salt
- 1/2 teaspoon ground allspice
- 1/2 teaspoon ground cloves
- 1/2 teaspoon ground cinnamon

Directions:

1. To prepare the tomatoes: Boil a pot of water over high heat. While boiling the water, make an 'X' on the bottom of each tomato using a paring knife.
2. Have a bowl of ice water on your countertop near the stovetop. Drop the tomatoes carefully into the pot of boiling water, and let them cook for a minute. Soon you can see a bit of loose skin around the area of the 'X' on the tomatoes.
3. Lift the tomatoes with a slotted spoon, one or two at a time, drop them into the bowl of ice water and leave them to cool.
4. Peel off the skin and chop them.
5. Measure out 5 cups and add into a stainless saucepan. Stir in cayenne pepper, sugar, and onion.
6. Place the saucepan over medium heat. Keep stirring all the while until it starts boiling. Turn the heat to low and let it boil gently for about 20 minutes. Stir on and off. Turn off the heat.
7. Pour the mixture into a food mill and strain the mixture.
8. Pour the strained mixture into the saucepan. Add salt, vinegar, garlic, and spices and mix well.
9. Place the saucepan over high heat. When it starts boiling, turn down the heat and cook until the preferred thickness is reached. Remember, the sauce will thicken on cooling. Stir it often.
10. Pour sauce into the jars. Let there be 1/4 inch of empty space

on top of the jars. After removing the bubbles, seal the jars.

11. Process the jars for 10 minutes in a boiling water bath, adjusting for altitude if required.

Hot Pepper Sauce

Yields: 4 half-pint jars

Ingredients:

- 1 pound peppers, chopped into chunks (use a mixture of sweet peppers and hot peppers, deseed if you do not want it hot)
- 1 cup white vinegar
- 1 teaspoon garlic powder
- 1 teaspoon ground mustard
- 1 teaspoon sea salt
- 1/2 teaspoon ground allspice
- 1 cup apple cider vinegar
- 1 cup chopped onion
- 1 teaspoon ground cumin
- 1 teaspoon turmeric powder
- 1/2 teaspoon ground cloves
- 4 teaspoons sugar

Directions:

1. Add peppers, white vinegar, apple cider vinegar, sugar, spices, salt, and onions into a stockpot.
2. Place the pot over medium heat. Stir often until the sugar dissolves completely and starts boiling.
3. Bring the heat to low and let it simmer for 20 – 25 minutes.
4. Turn off the heat. Pass the mixture through a food mill. Blending the mixture in a blender will give a smooth sauce. Reheat if necessary.
5. Ladle the sauce into the jars having 1/4 inch of empty space

on top of the jars, and removing the bubbles. Seal the jars.

6. Immerse the jars in the boiling water bath and process for 10 minutes. Adjust the time for higher altitude.

Creole Sauce

Yields: 4 – 5 half-pint jars

Ingredients:

- 2 3/4 pounds tomatoes
- 1/2 cup chopped green onions (both white and green)
- 2 cloves garlic, peeled, minced
- 1/2 tablespoon dried oregano
- 1/2 teaspoon black pepper
- 1/2 chopped green pepper
- 2 tablespoons red wine vinegar
- 1 tablespoon Worcestershire sauce
- 1 teaspoon hot pepper sauce
- 1/4 teaspoon salt or to taste
- 1/4 teaspoon cayenne pepper

Directions:

1. To prepare the tomatoes: Boil a pot of water over high heat. While boiling the water, make an 'X' on the bottom of each tomato using a sharp kitchen knife.

2. Have a bowl of ice water on your countertop near the stovetop. Put the tomatoes carefully into the pot of boiling water, and cook them for about a minute or until you see a bit of loose skin around the area of the 'X' on the tomatoes.

3. Remove the tomatoes with a slotted spoon, one or two at a time, and drop them into the bowl of ice water. Let the tomatoes remain in this bowl for a while to cool.

4. Peel off the skin from the tomatoes over a bowl so that any juice while peeling can be collected.

5. Chop the peeled tomatoes.

6. Measure out 2 3/4 cups and add into a stainless saucepan. Stir in cayenne pepper, salt, pepper, hot pepper sauce, oregano, Worcestershire sauce, garlic, vinegar, green pepper, and onion.

7. Place the saucepan over high heat. Upon boiling, turn the heat to medium and cook for about 25 – 30 minutes. Stir on and off.

8. Pour sauce into the jars leaving 1/4 inch space on top of the jars. After debubbling, seal the jars.

9. Process the jars in the prepared canner for 10 minutes. Adjust for altitude if required.

☆ ☆ ☆ ☆ ☆

Water Bath Canning
Tomato Recipes

Canning Tomatoes

Yields: 3 quarts and 1-pint size jars

Ingredients:

- 11 pounds tomatoes
- 1 teaspoon salt per quart-size jar (optional)
- 2 tablespoons bottled lemon juice per quart size jar or 1 tablespoon per pint size jar

Directions:

1. To prepare the tomatoes: Boil a pot of water over high heat. While the water is boiling, make an 'X' on the bottom of each tomato.
2. Have a bowl of ice water ready on your countertop near the stovetop. Drop the tomatoes carefully into the pot of boiling water. Let the tomatoes cook for a minute. Soon you can see a bit of loose skin around the area of the 'X' on the tomatoes.
3. Lift the tomatoes with a slotted spoon, one or two at a time, drop them into the bowl of ice water, and leave them to cool off for a while.
4. Peel off the skin of the tomatoes and remove their core (the area of the stem) with a knife.
5. Place the peeled and cored tomatoes in the same bowl.
6. Add salt and lemon juice to each jar. Fill the jars with tomatoes, leaving 1/2 inch of space on top of the jars.
7. Larger tomatoes can be halved or quartered to push into the jars.
8. If there is more headspace, pour any collected juice from the bowl of tomatoes into the jars. After pouring the juice, pour some boiling water if there is still extra space left.
9. Dissipate the bubbles before sealing the jars.
10. The jars are to be processed in the water bath canner for 85 minutes. Adjust the timing for altitude.

☆ ☆ ☆ ☆ ☆

Tomato Paste

Yields: 4 – 5 half-pint jars

Ingredients:

- 7 pounds Roma tomatoes or paste-type tomatoes, rinsed, cored, chopped about 1/4 – 1/2 inch pieces
- 1 bay leaf
- 2 small cloves garlic, peeled (optional)
- 1/2 teaspoon citric acid
- 1/2 teaspoon canning or pickling salt

Directions:

1. Place the tomatoes in a saucepan and place it over high heat.
2. Cook covered until it begins to boil. Make sure to stir often.
3. When the tomatoes start boiling, turn down the heat and cook for about 30 to 40 minutes. As it cooks, stir it on and off.
4. Turn off the heat and pass the tomatoes into a food mill or strainer in batches and strain the tomatoes. Discard the solids.
5. Pour the strained tomatoes into the saucepan. Stir in citric acid. Do not skip adding citric acid. It is very important. The citric acid is added only after straining the tomatoes. Make sure about this.
6. Stir well so that citric acid dissolves completely. Stir in salt, garlic, and bay leaf. Place the saucepan over medium heat and cook for about 60 to 90 minutes or half the quantity after straining the tomatoes.
7. While the tomato paste is cooking, during the last 30 minutes, arrange the water bath canner.
8. Spoon the tomato paste into the jars leaving 1/2 inch space on top of the jars, removing bubbles. Seal the jars.
9. The jars are to be immersed in a water bath canner for 45 minutes. Adjust the timing according to the altitude you live in.

Tomato Juice

Yields: 4-pint jars or 2-quart size jars

Ingredients:

- 6 – 6 1/2 pounds of tomatoes
- 1/2 teaspoon salt per pint size jar or 1 teaspoon per quart size jar
- 2 tablespoons bottled lemon juice per quart size jar or 1 tablespoon per pint size jar OR 1/4 teaspoon citric acid per pint size jar or 1/2 teaspoon citric acid per quart size jar

Directions:

1. Rinse the tomatoes well. Remove any stems or leaves from the tomatoes. Cut about a pound of tomatoes into 4 quarters each and place them in a large saucepan. Place the saucepan over high heat. Continue quartering the tomatoes about a pound at a time and keep adding them to the pot. Be quick while cutting and adding.
2. Stir as you add tomatoes and mash the tomatoes with the back of a large stirring spoon or potato masher. When all the tomatoes are added, wait for them to boil. Make sure to stir often.
3. Once all of it is added, let it cook on medium heat for about 5 minutes.
4. Turn off the heat and pass the tomatoes into a food mill or strainer in batches and strain the tomatoes. Discard the solids.
5. Pour the strained tomatoes into the saucepan. Place it over high heat and let it come to a boil.
6. Meanwhile, add salt and citric acid to each jar. Do not skip adding citric acid. It is very important.
7. Pour the juice into the jars leaving 1/4 inch of space on top of

the jars. Seal the jars on debubbling.

8. Put the jars in the water bath canner and process for 35 minutes using pint jars or 40 minutes using quart jars and adjust for altitude if required.

Pizza Sauce

Yields: 3 – 4 half-pint size jars

Ingredients:

- 4 pounds fresh tomatoes
- 3 teaspoons white vinegar
- 1/2 teaspoon sugar or more if you like it sweeter
- 1 cup olive oil
- 12 cloves garlic, peeled, finely chopped, crushed into a paste
- 1/2 teaspoon salt
- 1/2 teaspoon pepper

Directions:

1. Boil the water in a pot over high heat and add the tomatoes. Let it boil for about 5 – 8 minutes or until you can remove the skin easily.
2. Drain the tomatoes and place them in a bowl. Mash them up and strain them either through a food mill or a strainer. Discard the solids.
3. Pour the strained mixture into the pot. Add garlic, sugar, salt, oil, and pepper, and Whisk until smooth. If the sauce has gone cold, reheat.
4. Fill the sauce into the jars. Let there be 1/4 inch of empty space on top of the jars, and remove the bubbles. Seal the jars.
5. Submerge the jars in the boiling water bath and boil for 20 minutes. Seal the jars after debubbling. Adjust time for altitude.

6. Let the jars cool for 24 hours.

Bruschetta in a Jar

Yields: 3 – 4 half-pint jars

Ingredients:

- 4 1/2 cups cored, diced tomatoes (1-inch dice)
- 1/2 cup dry white wine
- 1/4 cup sugar
- 1 tablespoon dried oregano
- 1 tablespoon dried basil
- 1 tablespoon balsamic vinegar
- 2 – 3 cloves garlic, peeled, finely chopped
- 1/2 cup white wine vinegar
- 1 tablespoon sugar
- 1 tablespoon dried oregano

Directions:

1. Add sugar, garlic, water, herbs, wine, balsamic, and wine vinegar into a pot and place it over high heat.
2. Let it come to a rapid boil. Stir on and off. Turn the heat to low and cook covered for 3 – 4 minutes. Turn off the heat.
3. Place the tomatoes into the prepared jars and pack them tightly. Leave 1/2 inch of space from the top of the jars.
4. Pour the vinegar mixture into the jars. Leave 1/2 inch of space on top of the jars. Seal the jars after removing the bubbles.
5. Process the jars in the prepared canner for 20 minutes. Adjust for altitude if required.

Tomato Taco Sauce

Yields: 2 quarts

Ingredients:

- 4 quarts peeled, cored, finely chopped tomatoes (paste-type tomatoes)
- 2 1/2 cups chopped onions
- 2 long green chilies, deseeded, chopped
- 1 tablespoon salt
- 1/2 tablespoon sugar
- 1/2 teaspoon ground cumin (optional)
- 1 clove garlic, crushed
- 2 jalapeño peppers, deseeded, chopped
- 1 1/4 cups vinegar (5%)
- 3/4 tablespoon pepper
- 1 tablespoon oregano leaves (optional)

Directions:

1. Add all the ingredients into a saucepan and stir. Place the saucepan over high heat. Stir often until it starts boiling.
2. Turn the heat to low and cook until thick. Turn off the heat.
3. Pour sauce into the jars leaving 1/2 inch space on top of the jars, removing bubbles. Seal the jars.
4. Immerse the jars in the water bath and process for 15 minutes.

Spaghetti Sauce

Yields: 4 – 5 quart size jars or 8 – 10 pint size jars

Ingredients:

- 12.5 pounds tomatoes
- 2 large onions, finely chopped

- 2 tablespoons canola oil
- 1/8 cup salt
- 2 large green bell peppers, deseeded, finely chopped
- 1 can (12 ounces) tomato paste
- 1/3 cup sugar
- 4 cloves garlic, minced
- 1 teaspoon dried parsley flakes
- 1 teaspoon crushed pepper flakes
- 1 bay leaf
- 2 teaspoons dried oregano
- 1 teaspoon dried basil
- 1 teaspoon Worcestershire sauce
- 2 tablespoons bottled or fresh lemon juice per quart-size jar or 1 tablespoon per pint-sizejar

Directions:

1. To prepare the tomatoes: Boil a pot of water over high heat. While the water is boiling, make an 'X' on the bottom of each tomato using a paring knife.
2. Have a bowl of ice water ready on your countertop near the stovetop. Drop the tomatoes carefully into the pot of boiling water. Let the tomatoes cook for a minute. Soon you can see a bit of loose skin around the area of the 'X' on the tomatoes.
3. Pick the tomatoes with a slotted spoon, one or two at a time, and drop them into the bowl of ice water. Let the tomatoes remain in this bowl for a while to cool.
4. Peel the tomatoes and core them with a knife.
5. Place the peeled and cored tomatoes in the same bowl.
6. Set aside the lemon juice and add the ingredients to a large pot.
7. Pour enough water to cover the ingredients in the pot. You can use cooked tomato water instead of plain water.
8. Boil the mixture over medium-high heat.
9. Turn down the heat and boil gently without covering the pot

for about 3 to 4 hours,stirring on and off.

10. Take out the bay leaf and discard.

11. Pour lemon juice into each jar.

12. Ladle sauce into the jars with 1/2 inch of empty space at the top of the bottles. Debubble before sealing the jars.

13. Place the jars in the water bath canner and process for 40 minutes. Accordingly change the timing for higher altitude.

Water Bath Canning Salsa Recipes

Salsa

Yields: 3 – 4 pint-size jars

Ingredients:

- 4 1/2 cups prepared tomatoes (about 4 – 5 pounds of tomatoes)
- 1 1/4 cups chopped white onion
- 4 large cloves garlic, peeled, chopped
- 1/2 cup white vinegar
- 1 1/4 cups chopped green bell peppers
- 2 medium jalapeños, chopped (add more if you like it hot)
- 3 teaspoons canning salt
- 1/2 can (from a 12 ounce can) of tomato paste

Directions:

1. To prepare the tomatoes: To prepare the tomatoes: Boil a pot of water over high heat. While the water is boiling, make an 'X' on the bottom of each tomato using a paring knife.
2. Have a bowl of ice water ready on your countertop near the stovetop. Drop the tomatoes carefully into the pot of boiling water. Let the tomatoes cook for a minute. Soon you can see a bit of loose skin around the area of the 'X' on the tomatoes.
3. Pick out the tomatoes with a slotted spoon, one or two at a time, and drop them into the bowl of ice water. Let the tomatoes remain in this bowl for a while to cool.
4. Peel off the skin from the tomatoes and core them with a knife.
5. Place the peeled and cored tomatoes in the same bowl.
6. Now chop the tomatoes.
7. Measure 4 ½ cups of tomatoes and add them to a pot.
8. Also, add onion, garlic, vinegar, bell peppers, jalapeños, salt, and tomato paste into the pot of tomatoes.
9. Place the pot over medium-high heat. Give it a good stir. Once it starts boiling, turn the heat to low and simmer until thick, stirring now and then. Turn off the heat.
10. Spoon the salsa into the jars, leaving 1/2 inch of space on top

of the jars, removing bubbles.

11. Submerge the jars in the boiling water bath and process for 30 minutes. Adjust for altitude if required.

12. After cooling the jars for 24 hours, set them aside for storage.

13. If you prefer chunky salsa, chop the vegetables into chunks.

☆ ☆ ☆ ☆ ☆

Pico de Gallo

Yields: 8 half-pint jars

Ingredients:

- 4 pounds deseeded Roma tomatoes, rinsed, cored, deseeded, finely chopped
- 2 large jalapeño peppers, finely chopped
- 1 cup bottled lime juice
- 2 medium onions, finely chopped
- 1/4 cup chopped cilantro
- 2 teaspoons salt

Directions:

1. Combine the tomatoes, jalapeño, lime juice, onions, cilantro, and salt in a pot.

2. Place the pot over high heat. Stir often. When it starts boiling, turn down the heat and cook for about 3 minutes.

3. Turn off the heat.

4. Fill the salsa into the jars. Leave 1/2 inch of free space on top of the jars, removing bubbles. You can seal the jars now.

5. Immerse the jars in the prepared canner and process for 15 minutes. Adjust the timing for higher altitude.

☆ ☆ ☆ ☆ ☆

Summer Salsa

Yields: 4 half-pint size jars

Ingredients:

- 2 cups prepared tomatoes (about 2 pounds)
- 1/2 red bell pepper, diced
- 2 jalapeño peppers, deseed if desired, finely chopped
- 1/4 cup honey
- 1/8 cup balsamic vinegar
- 2 cups pitted, peeled, chopped peaches
- 1/2 cup chopped red onion
- 1/4 cup finely chopped cilantro
- Juice of 1/2 lemon
- Zest of 1/2 lemon, grated

Directions:

1. To prepare the tomatoes: To prepare the tomatoes: Boil a pot of water over high heat. While boiling the water, make an 'X' on the bottom of each tomato using a paring knife.
2. Have a bowl of ice water on your countertop near the stovetop. Drop the tomatoes carefully into the pot of boiling water. Let the tomatoes cook for a minute. Soon you can see a bit of loose skin around the area of the 'X' on the tomatoes.
3. Lift the tomatoes with a slotted spoon, one or two at a time, and drop them into the bowl of ice water. Let the tomatoes remain in this bowl for a while to cool.
4. Peel off the skin from the tomatoes over a bowl so that any juice while peeling can be collected, then core them with a knife.
5. Add the peeled and cored tomatoes into the same bowl.
6. Chop the tomatoes.
7. Measure 2 cups of tomatoes and add into a Dutch oven or stainless steel pot.
8. Add peppers, peaches, and onions to the pot of tomatoes. Give

it a good stir and place it over medium heat.

9. Stir constantly until the mixture starts boiling.

10. Stir in the lemon zest, cilantro, lemon juice, honey, and vinegar, stirring often.

11. When the mixture starts boiling again, turn the heat low and cook until slightly thick. Stir often. Turn off the heat.

12. Ladle the salsa into the jars with empty space of 1/2 inch on top of the jars. Seal the jars after removing the bubbles.

13. Process the jars for 15 minutes in a boiling water bath with adjustment for altitude if necessary.

Corn Salsa

Yields: 2 – 3 pint-size jars

Ingredients:

- 3 ears of corn on the cob
- 1 small yellow onion, diced
- 1 small jalapeño pepper, minced
- 2 small cloves garlic, minced
- 1/4 large green bell pepper, diced
- 1 1/4 pounds tomatoes, diced
- 1/4 very small habanero pepper, minced
- 10 tablespoons white vinegar
- 2 tablespoons sugar
- 3/4 teaspoon ground cumin
- 2 tablespoons lime juice
- 3/4 teaspoon salt
- 1/8 cup chopped fresh cilantro

Directions:

1. Preheat your grill to medium heat and grill the corn until lightly charred. Turn the corn now and then.

2. Let the corn cool slightly. Remove the corn kernels using a knife.

3. Add vinegar, sugar, lime juice, cumin, and salt into a Dutch oven or stainless steel heavy pot and place the pot over high heat. Stir often.

4. When it starts boiling, stir in the grilled corn, peppers, onion, tomatoes, and garlic. When it begins to boil, turn the heat to low and cook for about 5 minutes or until slightly thick. Stir often.

5. Stir in cilantro and mix well. Heat thoroughly. Turn off the heat.

6. Fill the salsa into the jars with 1/2 inch of headspace. After removing the bubbles, seal the jars.

7. Submerge the jars in the water bath canner and boil for 15 minutes. Adjust the time for higher altitudes if required.

Fresh Vegetable Salsa

Yields: 5 half-pint jars

Ingredients:

- 3 1/2 cups prepared tomatoes (about 3 pounds of tomatoes)
- 1/2 cup coarsely chopped green bell pepper
- 2 cloves garlic, minced
- 6 tablespoons white vinegar
- 1/4 teaspoon ground cumin
- 1 cup coarsely chopped onions
- 4 jalapeño peppers, chopped
- 2.6 ounces tomato paste
- 1/4 cup lightly packed chopped cilantro

Directions:

1. To prepare the tomatoes: To prepare the tomatoes: Boil a pot

of water over high heat. While boiling the water, make an 'X' on the bottom of each tomato using a small, sharp knife.

2. Have a bowl of ice water ready on your countertop near the stovetop. Drop the tomatoes carefully into the pot of boiling water. Let the tomatoes cook for a minute until the skin begins to loosen around the area of the 'X' on the tomatoes.

3. Lift the tomatoes with a slotted spoon, one or two at a time, and drop them into the bowl of ice water. Let the tomatoes remain in this bowl for a while to cool.

4. Peel the tomatoes and core them with a knife.

5. Place the peeled and cored tomatoes in the same bowl.

6. Chop the tomatoes.

7. Measure 3 1/2 cups of tomatoes and add into a Dutch oven or stainless steel pot.

8. Add onions, jalapeño, tomato paste, cilantro, green pepper, garlic, vinegar, and cumin into the pot of tomatoes. Place the pot over high heat.

9. Stir often. When it starts boiling, turn the heat to low and cook until you get the preferred thickness. Remember, it will thicken further on cooling.

10. Turn off the heat.

11. Ladle the salsa into the jars. Make sure to have 1/2 inch of empty space on the top of the jars, debubble and seal the jars.

12. Place the jars in the prepared canner and process for 15 minutes. Adjust the timing for higher altitudes.

Mango Salsa

Yields: 3 half-pint jars

Ingredients:

- 3 cups diced, raw (unripe and green) mangoes
- 1/4 cup finely chopped yellow onion

- 1 teaspoon finely chopped garlic
- 1/2 cup light brown sugar
- 1/4 cup water
- 3/4 cup diced red bell pepper
- 1/4 teaspoon crushed red pepper flakes
- 1 teaspoon finely chopped ginger
- 10 tablespoons cider vinegar (5% acidity)

Directions:

1. It is recommended to wear gloves while chopping the mangoes. Cut them into 1/2 inch dice.
2. Add mangoes, onion, garlic, sugar, water, bell pepper, red pepper flakes, ginger, and vinegar into a Dutch oven or pot. Place the pot over high heat. Stir often until the sugar dissolves.
3. When it starts boiling, turn the heat to low and cook for about 5 minutes.
4. Turn off the heat.
5. Remove salsa with a slotted spoon and add into the jars. 1/2 inch of empty space is to be left on top of the jars.
6. Pour the liquid into the jars, maintaining 1/2 inch space and removing the bubbles. Seal the jars.
7. The jars are to be processed in the boiling water bath for 15 minutes with adjustment of time for altitude.

Peach Salsa

Yields: 4 half-pint jars

Ingredients:

- 2 jalapeño peppers, deseed if desired, finely chopped
- 1 tablespoon honey
- 3 cups pitted, peeled peach chunks

- 1/4 cup white vinegar (5% or stronger)
- 3.5 ounces onion, chopped
- 1/2 red bell pepper, diced
- 2 small cloves garlic, minced
- 1/4 teaspoon cayenne pepper
- 1 tablespoon bottled lime juice
- 1/4 cup finely chopped cilantro
- 3/4 teaspoon ground cumin

Directions:

1. Add peppers, peaches, garlic, spices, cilantro, lime juice, vinegar, honey, and onions into a pot or Dutch oven. Give it a good stir and place it over medium heat.
2. Stir constantly until the mixture starts boiling.
3. When the mixture starts boiling again, turn the heat low and cook until slightly thick. Stir often. Turn off the heat.
4. Spoon the salsa into the jars, leaving 1/2 inch of space on top of the jars, removing bubbles. Seal the jars.
5. Submerge the jars in the water bath canner and process for 15 minutes. Adjust the timing if you live at higher altitudes.
6. Let the jars cool for 24 hours.

☆ ☆ ☆ ☆ ☆

Cranberry Salsa

Yields: 2 – 3 half-pint size jars

Ingredients:

- 2 cups coarsely chopped fresh or frozen cranberries
- 1/2 cup chopped red onion
- 2 – 4 tablespoons honey, to taste
- 2 tablespoons lemon juice
- 1/2 teaspoon pickling salt
- 1/2 cup dried cranberries

- 1/4 cup chopped fresh parsley
- 2 tablespoons red wine vinegar
- 4 teaspoons granulated sugar
- 1/2 teaspoon red pepper flakes

Directions:

1. Add cranberries, onion, honey, lemon juice, pickling salt, parsley, vinegar, sugar, and red pepper flakes into a saucepan.
2. Cook the mixture over medium heat. When it starts boiling, turn the heat to low and cook until thick. Stir often. Turn off the heat.
3. Fill the salsa into the jars. Make sure to have 1/2 inch of space from the top. Make sure to dissipate the bubbles before sealing the jars.
4. The jars are to be processed in the water bath canner for 20 minutes. Adjust for altitude if required.

Pineapple Papaya Chili Salsa

Yields: 3 half-pint jars

Ingredients:

- 2 cups cubed, deseeded peeled papaya
- 1/2 cup golden raisins
- 1/4 cup lemon juice
- 1/4 cup pineapple juice
- 1/4 cup lime juice
- 1/4 cup chopped, deseeded Anaheim peppers or Poblano or banana peppers, or New Mexico chilies
- 1 tablespoon finely chopped cilantro
- 1 cup peeled, cored, cubed fresh pineapple
- 1 tablespoon finely chopped green onion
- 1 tablespoon packed brown sugar

Directions:

1. Add papaya, raisins, peppers, cilantro, pineapple, green onion, brown sugar, and all the juices into a stainless steel saucepan.
2. Place the saucepan over medium-high heat. Stir all the time until it starts boiling.
3. Turn down the heat and cook for 5 – 8 minutes or until slightly thick.
4. Turn off the heat.
5. Transfer the salsa into the jars, leaving 1/2 inch of space on top of the jars. Seal the jars after debubbling.
6. Immerse the jars in the boiling water bath and boil for 20 minutes. Adjust the time for different altitudes.

Water Bath Canning Pickle Recipes

Cucumber and Lemon Pickles

Yields: 3 pint jars

Ingredients:

- 4 large cucumbers, peeled, chopped into 1/2-inch chunks
- 1 tablespoon pickling salt
- 11 tablespoons white vinegar
- 6 tablespoons fresh lemon juice
- 1/2 tablespoon whole peppercorns
- 1/2 lemon, cut into slices
- 2 sweet red bell peppers, deseeded, sliced
- Ice water, as required
- 4 tablespoons granulated sugar
- 2 small bay leaves
- 1/2 teaspoon allspice berries
- 3 cloves garlic, peeled

Directions:

1. Place the cucumbers and bell peppers in a bowl. Add salt and mix well. Pour enough ice water to cover the cucumbers and peppers. Set aside the bowl for about 3 hours.
2. Add sugar, vinegar, and lemon juice into a saucepan.
3. Place a bay leaf, allspice, and peppercorns on a piece of cheesecloth and tie it up.
4. Drop the spice bag into the saucepan and place it over high heat.
5. As it starts boiling, turn the heat to low and let it boil gently for about 6 – 7 minutes.
6. Drain the vegetables in a colander and add to the saucepan with a hot solution. When it starts boiling once again, turn off the heat.
7. Meanwhile, add a bay leaf, a clove of garlic, and a lemon slice into each prepared jar.

8. Remove the cucumbers and bell pepper with a slotted spoon and place the strained vegetables in jars, leaving 3/4 inch of headspace.

9. Pour the hot solution into the jars until you get 1/2 inch of headspace. Seal the jars after debubbling.

10. Process the jars in the prepared canner for 10 minutes. Adjust for altitude if required. Let the jars cool for 24 hours.

Sweet Gherkin Pickles

Yields: 3 – 4 pint jars

Ingredients:

- 3 1/2 pounds gherkins, about 1 1/2 inches long (baby cucumbers)
- 4 cups sugar
- 1/2 teaspoon turmeric powder
- 1 teaspoon whole mixed pickling spice
- 1/4 teaspoon fennel (optional)
- 1/4 cup canning or pickling salt
- 3 cups 5% vinegar
- 1 teaspoon celery seeds
- 1 stick cinnamon
- 1 teaspoon vanilla extract (optional)
- Boiling water, as required

Directions:

1. **Day 1**: Cut a thin slice, about 1/16 of an inch, from the bottom end of the cucumbers. Do not cut from the stem side, and make sure the cucumbers have about 1/4 inch of the stem attached. Place them in a container.

2. Pour enough boiling water over the cucumbers. Let the

cucumbers soak for 6 – 8 hours.

3. **Day 2**: Drain off the water from the cucumbers and pour 3 quarts of boiling water (to which 2 tablespoons of salt is added) over the cucumbers.

4. **Day 3**: Drain off the water from the cucumbers. Take a fork, pierce the cucumbers at a few places, and then place them back in the container.

5. Add 1 1/2 cups sugar, 1 1/2 cups vinegar, turmeric, cinnamon, and celery seeds into a saucepan and place the saucepan over medium heat.

6. When the solution starts boiling, turn off the heat and pour the solution over the cucumbers. Let it soak for about 8 hours.

7. Place a colander over a bowl and strain the cucumbers in the colander. Retain the solution.

8. Pour the solution back into the saucepan. Add 1 cup sugar and 1 cup vinegar into the saucepan and place the saucepan over high heat. When it boils, turn off the heat and pour over the cucumbers. Let it soak until the next day.

9. **Day 4**: Place a colander over a bowl and strain the cucumbers in the colander. Retain the solution. Pour it back into the saucepan.

10. Add 1 cup sugar and 1/2 cup vinegar into the saucepan and place the saucepan over high heat. When it boils, turn off the heat and pour over the cucumbers. Let them soak for 6 – 8 hours.

11. Place a colander over a bowl and strain the cucumbers in the colander. Retain the solution, pouring it back into the saucepan. Stir in ½ cup sugar and vanilla extract.

12. Place the saucepan over high heat. When the solution starts boiling, turn off the heat.

13. Pack the cucumbers in the jars. Pour the hot solution over the cucumbers. Leave ½ inch of empty space from the rim of the jars. Remove the bubbles before sealing the jars.

14. Plunge the jars into the boiling water bath and boil for 5

minutes. Adjust the timing if you live at a higher altitude. Let the jars cool for 24 hours.

Pickled Sweet Green Tomatoes

Yields: 4 – 5 pint jars

Ingredients:

- 5 – 6 pounds green tomatoes (8 cups sliced)
- 2 tablespoons canning salt or pickling salt
- 2 cups 5% vinegar
- 1/2 tablespoon allspice berries
- 1/2 tablespoon whole cloves
- 1 cup sliced onions
- 1 1/2 cups brown sugar
- 1/2 tablespoon mustard seeds
- 1/2 tablespoon celery seeds

Directions:

1. Combine onions, tomatoes, and salt in a bowl. Set aside for 4 – 6 hours.
2. Drain the liquid and add the tomato mixture into a saucepan. Add vinegar and sugar and place the saucepan over medium heat. Stir often until the sugar dissolves.
3. Place the whole spices in a cheesecloth piece and tie it into a bag. Drop the bag into the saucepan. The liquid in the saucepan should cover the tomatoes. If it does not, add some water to cover it. Place the saucepan over medium heat. Upon boiling, turn the heat to low and let it bubble until the tomatoes are soft. Stir on and off.
4. Discard the spice bag.
5. Remove the tomatoes and onions with a slotted spoon and add the strained tomatoes into the jars. Pour the hot solution into

the jars, leaving 1/2 inch of free space at the top. Remove the bubbles. Seal the jars.

6. Dip the jars in the boiling water bath and process for 10 minutes, adjusting for altitude if required. Let the jars cool for 24 hours.

Marrow and Onion Mustard Pickles

Yields: 3-pint jars

Ingredients:

- 6 cups prepared vegetable marrow cubes (about 2 1/2 - 3 pounds unpeeled marrow)
- 4 cups small pickling or pearl onions
- 3 tablespoons all-purpose flour
- 3/4 teaspoon celery seeds
- 1/4 cup water
- 1 large hot red pepper or Shepherd sweet pepper, deseeded, chopped
- 2 tablespoons pickling salt
- 14 tablespoons granulated sugar
- 3 tablespoons mustard seeds
- 3/4 teaspoon turmeric powder
- 1 cup white vinegar

Directions:

1. To prepare the marrow: Remove the peel from the marrow and cut it into 2 halves.
2. Remove the seeds and membranes and chop them into 3/4-inch cubes.
3. Place a layer of marrow cubes in a glass container. Sprinkle some salt over it. Repeat these layers of marrow and salt until

it is used up. Cover the bowl and keep it aside for 2 – 4 hours.

4. To prepare the onions: Boil a small pot of water. Drop the onions into the pot and drain off after about a minute. When they cool down, peel the onions.

5. Add sugar, turmeric, mustard seeds, flour, and celery seeds into a stainless steel saucepan.

6. Add water and whisk well. Add vinegar and hot red pepper and whisk well. Place the saucepan over high heat. Stir continuously until the mixture is thick.

7. Stir the marrow and onions in and turn off the heat when the mixture starts boiling.

8. Spoon the pickles into the jars. Let there be 1/2 inch of empty space at the neck of the jars. Seal the jars after debubbling.

9. Dunk the jars in the prepared canner and boil for 15 minutes, adjusting for altitude if required. Let them cool for 24 hours.

Zucchini Pickles

Yields: 3-pint jars

Ingredients:

- 7 cups prepared zucchini (about 2 1/4 pounds whole zucchini)
- 3 cups white vinegar
- 2 teaspoons mustard seeds
- 1 teaspoon turmeric powder
- 1/4 cup pickling salt
- 2 cups granulated sugar
- 1 teaspoon celery seeds

Directions:

1. Rinse and trim the ends of the zucchini. Cut into 1/4-inch thick slices on the diagonal.

2. Place a layer of zucchini in a glass container. Sprinkle some

salt over it. Repeat these layers of zucchini and salt until all of it is used up. Pour enough cold water to cover the zucchini. Cover the bowl and keep it aside for 2 hours.

3. Add zucchini in a colander. Once the water is drained, rinse it under cold running water. Make sure you rinse thoroughly.

4. Dry the zucchini by patting it with a towel or paper towel.

5. Add sugar, vinegar, and spices into a stainless steel saucepan. Place the saucepan over high heat. When it starts boiling, turn the heat to low and cook for about 5 minutes.

6. Turn off the heat. Add zucchini and let it rest for an hour.

7. Now prepare the canner.

8. Place the pot over high heat. Once it starts boiling, turn the heat to low and let it boil gently t for about 5 minutes. Turn off the heat.

9. Remove the zucchini with a perforated spoon and place it in the jars.

10. Pour the hot solution into the jars. Let there be 1/2 inch of empty space left on top of the jars. Seal the jars after debubbling.

11. Submerge the jars in the prepared canner and let it boil for 10 minutes. Adjust the time for higher altitudes. Let them cool for 24 hours.

Pickled 3 Bean Salad

Yields: 3 pint jars

Ingredients:

- 2 1/4 cups trimmed, cut green beans (about 1 1/2 inch long pieces)
- 1/2 pound lima beans, shelled
- 2 1/4 cups trimmed, cut yellow wax beans (about 1 1/2 inch long pieces)

- 1 cup chopped celery (3/4 inch long pieces)
- 1/2 cup diced, deseeded red bell pepper
- 3/4 cup sliced red onions
- 2 1/4 cups granulated sugar
- 1/2 teaspoon celery seeds
- 1 1/2 cups white vinegar
- 1/2 tablespoon mustard seeds
- 2 teaspoons pickling or canning salts
- 5 ounces water

Directions:

1. Add all the beans, onions, celery, and bell pepper into a saucepan. Pour boiling water over the vegetables. Place the saucepan over medium heat.
2. When the mixture starts boiling, turn down the heat and let it simmer for about 5 minutes.
3. Add vinegar, salt, sugar, water, mustard, and celery seeds into another saucepan. Place the saucepan over medium heat.
4. Stir often until the sugar dissolves completely. When the mixture starts boiling, turn down the heat and let it simmer for about 5 minutes.
5. Remove the vegetables using a large spoon with holes in them and place them in the jars.
6. Pour the brine into the jars, leaving 1/2 inch of empty space on top of the jars. After removing the bubbles, seal the jars.
7. Dip the jars in the boiling water bath for 10 minutes. Change the timing for a higher altitude. Let the jars cool for 24 hours.

Marinated Whole Mushrooms

Yields: 4 – 5 half-pint jars

Ingredients:

- 3 1/2 pounds small whole mushrooms (about 1-inch diameter), rinsed
- 1 cup olive oil or salad oil
- 1/2 tablespoon oregano leaves
- 1/2 tablespoon canning or pickling salt
- 1/8 cup diced pimento
- 12 – 15 whole black peppercorns
- 1/4 cup bottled lemon juice
- 1 1/4 cups white vinegar (5%)
- 1/2 tablespoon dried basil leaves
- 1/4 cup finely chopped onions
- 1 clove garlic, quartered

Directions:

1. Leave about 1/4 inch of the stem and cut off the remaining part of the stem from the mushrooms.
2. Place the mushrooms in a saucepan. Cover with water. Stir in the lemon juice.
3. Place the saucepan over high heat. When the mixture starts boiling, turn down the heat and cook for about 4 – 5 minutes.
4. Drain off the mushrooms in a colander and add them back into the saucepan.
5. Add oil, salt, vinegar, and herbs and mix well. Add pimento and onions and mix well.
6. Place the saucepan over high heat. When it starts boiling, turn off the heat.
7. Put one piece of garlic into each jar. Divide the peppercorns equally and put them into the jars.
8. Remove the vegetables with a perforated spoon and place the

vegetables in the jars.

9. Pour the hot brine into the jars. Leave 1/2 inch of free space on top of the jars. Seal the jars after dissipating the bubbles.

10. Process the jars in the prepared canner for 20 minutes. Adjust for altitude if required. Let them cool for 24 hours.

Water Bath Canning Low Sugar/Sugar-free Recipes

Sweet Cucumber Slices

Yields: 2 – 3 pint jars

Ingredients:

- 1 3/4 pounds pickling cucumbers
- 2 cups cider vinegar (5%)
- 1/2 tablespoon canning salt
- 1/2 tablespoon mustard seeds
- 1/2 tablespoon celery seeds
- 1/2 tablespoon allspice berries
- 2 inch stick of cinnamon, broken into 2 – 3 pieces
- Boiling water, as required
- 1 1/2 cups Splenda
- 1/2 cup water

Directions:

1. Cut off about 1/16 inch thick slice from the bottom end of the cucumber (opposite the stem end)
2. Cut the cucumber into 1/4-inch thick slices lengthwise.
3. Place the cucumber slices in a bowl. Add boiling water to the bowl of cucumber to just cover the slices. Let them soak for 10 minutes.
4. Drain off the water. Rinse under cold water for a few minutes until the cucumbers are cold. Drain well.
5. Add vinegar, Splenda, 1/2 cup water, and spices into a saucepan. Stir often. Place the saucepan over high heat. When the mixture starts boiling, add cucumber and cook until it comes to a boil again. Turn off the heat.
6. Place one cinnamon piece into each jar. Remove cucumbers with a large spoon with holes and fill the cucumbers into the jars.
7. Pour the hot solution into the jars. Leave 1/2 inch of headspace.
8. On removing the bubbles, you can seal the jars. Put the jars in

the water bath canner and boil for 10 minutes. Adjust the timing for altitude if required.

No Sugar Added Pickled Beets

Yields: 4 pints

Ingredients:

- 3 1/2 pounds beets (about 2 – 2 1/2 inches diameter)
- 3 cups apple cider or white distilled vinegar (5%)
- 1 cup Splenda (optional)
- 1 stick cinnamon
- 2 – 3 onions (2 – 2 1/2 inches diameter), optional, thinly sliced
- 3/4 teaspoon canning or pickling salt
- 1 1/2 cups water
- 6 whole cloves

Directions:

1. Cut off most of the part of the stem and root of the beets, except about an inch.
2. Make sure the beets are of similar size.
3. Boil the beets in a pot of water until tender. Drain off the water. When the beets cool, remove whatever part of the stem and root that is remaining and peel off the skin.
4. Cut into 1/4-inch thick slices.
5. Add vinegar, Splenda, 1/2 cup water, and salt into a saucepan. Place the spices on a piece of cheesecloth and tie them up. Drop the spice bag into the saucepan over high heat. When the mixture starts boiling, add beets and onions and cook until they come to a boil again.
6. Turn the heat to low and cook for 5 minutes. Turn off the heat. Discard the spice bag.
7. Remove beets and onions with a slotted spoon and fill them

into the jars.

8. Pour the hot solution into the jars to fill up, leaving 1/2 inch of headspace. Seal the jars after removing the bubbles.

9. Place the jars in the boiling water bath and boil for 30 minutes. Adjust for altitude if required.

Low-Sugar Apple Chili Jam

Yields: 2 – 3 half-pint jars

Ingredients:

- 1 large apple, peeled, grated
- 2 cups apple juice
- 1/2 tablespoon crushed Chile de Arbol or crushed red pepper flakes
- 1/4 cup honey
- 1 1/2 tablespoons bottled lemon juice
- 1 1/2 tablespoons Ball Low or no-sugar pectin
- 1/4 cup sugar

Directions:

1. Add apple and lemon juice into a stainless steel pot or Dutch oven. Mix well and place the pot over medium heat. Keep stirring until the apples are cooked.

2. Turn up the heat to high heat, add apple juice, crushed chili, and pectin, and mix well. Let it come to a rapid boil.

3. Stir in the sugar and honey. Let it come to a rapid boil once again. Stir all the time.

4. Let it boil rapidly for a minute. Turn off the heat.

5. Spoon the jam into the jars, leaving space of 1/4 inch from the top of the jar., After removing the bubbles, you can seal the jars.

6. Immerse the jars in the water bath canner and process for 10

minutes. Adjust the time for higher altitudes.

Sugar-Free Raspberry Jam

Yields: 2 half-pint size jars

Ingredients:

- 2 cups mashed raspberries
- 1 teaspoon Pomona's pectin powder
- 1 tablespoon lemon juice
- 1 teaspoon calcium water
- 1/2 teaspoon vanilla
- 1. 6 tablespoons allulose

Directions:

1. To make calcium water, measure 1/4 teaspoon of calcium powder in the box of Pomona's pectin and add to a small jar. Pour ¼ cup water into the jar. Fasten the lid and shake the jar vigorously for a few seconds. Use only 1 teaspoon of the calcium water and store the remaining in the refrigerator. You can use it sometime later to make jelly or jam.
2. Mix the raspberries, lemon juice, and calcium water in a saucepan. Place the saucepan with raspberries over medium heat. Cook until slightly soft.
3. Meanwhile, combine pectin and allulose in a bowl.
4. Mash all the raspberries with a potato masher, according to the texture you prefer, smooth or chunky jam.
5. Stir in the pectin mixture and vanilla. Keep stirring until the mixture starts boiling. Let it boil hard for a minute. Turn off the heat. Remove any scum that may float on top.
6. Spoon the jam into jars. Have 1/4 inch of free space on top of the jars, and seal the jars after removing bubbles.
7. Process the jars for 10 minutes in a boiling water bath. Adjust

for altitude if required.

Low-Sugar Lemony Raspberry Jam

Yields: 3 half-pint jars

Ingredients:

- 1 3/4 pound fresh raspberries
- 2 tablespoons Ball Low or no-sugar pectin
- 1/4 cup fresh lemon juice
- 3/4 cup honey

Directions:

1. Crush the raspberries in a stainless steel pot or Dutch oven using a potato masher.
2. Add lemon juice and pectin and mix well. Place the pot over medium-high heat. Stir often. Add honey and mix well when the mixture comes to a rapid boil.
3. Let it come to a rapid boil once again. Now let it boil rapidly for exactly 1 minute.
4. Turn off the heat. Remove any scum that may float on top.
5. Fill the jam into jars with a headspace of 1/4 inch, removing the bubbles. Seal the jars.
6. Dunk the jars in the water bath canner and boil for 10 minutes. Adjust the time if you live at a higher altitude.

Low-Sugar Strawberry Tequila Agave Jam

Yields: 2 half-pint jars

Ingredients:

- 2 1/2 cups chopped fresh strawberries
- 2 1/2 tablespoons Ball Low or no-sugar pectin
- 1/4 cup tequila
- 1/2 cup agave syrup

Directions:

1. Mix the strawberries and tequila in a Dutch oven or stainless steel pot.
2. Using a potato masher, crush the strawberries.
3. Add pectin and stir. Place the pot over high heat. Let it come to a rapid boil, stirring all the time.
4. Add agave and mix well.
5. Let it come to a rapid boil once again. Now let it boil rapidly for exactly 1 minute. Keep stirring all the time.
6. Turn off the heat. Remove any scum that may float on top.
7. Transfer the jam into jars, leaving 1/4 inch of empty space at the top. Seal the jars after removing the bubbles.
8. Plunge the jars in the boiling water bath for 10 minutes. Adjust the timing for the altitude you live in.

☆ ☆ ☆ ☆ ☆

Sugar-Free Blackberry Jam

Yields: 2 half-pint size jars

Ingredients:

- 2 cups mashed blackberries

- 1 teaspoon Pomona's pectin powder
- 1/2 cup allulose
- 1 teaspoon calcium water
- 2 tablespoons lemon juice

Directions:

1. To make calcium water, mix 1/4 teaspoon of calcium powder (that is in the box of Pomona's pectin) with 1/4 cup of water in a small jar. Fasten the lid and shake the jar constantly until well incorporated. You need to use only 1 teaspoon of the mixture. Set the remaining calcium water aside in the refrigerator, and use it to make more jelly or jam when needed.
2. Add blackberries, lemon juice, and calcium water into a saucepan and mix well.
3. Place the saucepan over medium heat. Cook until slightly soft, stirring often.
4. Mash the blackberries with a potato masher and choose smooth jam or chunky mash jam, depending on your desired texture.
5. Combine pectin and allulose in a bowl and add to the pot. Mix well.
6. Keep stirring until the mixture starts boiling. Let it boil hard for a minute. Turn off the heat. Remove any scum that may float on top.
7. Spoon the jam into jars. Leave 1/4 inch of space from the rim of the jars, De bubble before sealing the jars
8. Process the jars in the water bath canner for 10 minutes. Adjust for altitude if required.

Sugar-free Blueberry Pie Filling

Yields: 5 – 6 pint jars

Ingredients:

- 4 cups water
- 1/2 teaspoon salt
- 1 cup ClearJel or Thermflo mixed with 1 cup cold water
- 2 1/2 tablespoons lemon juice
- 3/4 cup Gentle Sweet
- 1 cup cold water
- 8 cups fresh or frozen blueberries (thawed if frozen)

Directions:

1. Add water, salt, and Gentle Sweet into a pot and place it over high heat. Let it come to a boil.
2. Now add the ClearJel mixture, constantly stirring while adding. Turn the heat to low and cook until the mixture is transparent.
3. Turn off the heat. Add blueberries and lemon juice and mix well.
4. Spoon the filling into the prepared jars and pack them tightly. Leave headspace of 1 inch, removing the bubbles. Seal the jars.
5. Submerge the jars in the boiling water bath and process for 30 minutes. Adjust for altitude if required.

Conclusion

Home canning and preserving like the Amish are fun and productive, and I hope you think so too. Now you know what to do with your garden's extra produce.

This cookbook shares many delightful Amish recipes we hope you and your loved ones enjoy. Try each one out, and you will soon discover tastes you might have never tried. Don't restrict yourself to foods you only liked in the past. Home canned goods taste a lot better and are healthier than anything you might have bought from the store. So, give it a chance and discover tasty new food to add to your diet.

Canning is simple; you just need a few tries to get it right. As long as you follow canning recipes correctly, you are unlikely to fail. Use the tips and tricks in the book, and you will find it easier. So go buy those cans, pick your produce and begin canning!